The Crisis in
Higher Education

Other titles recently published under the SRHE/Open University Press imprint:

Michael Allen: *The Goals of Universities*
William Birch: *The Challenge to Higher Education*
Heather Eggins: *Restructuring Higher Education*
Colin Evans: *Language People*
Gunnar Handal and Per Lauvås: *Promoting Reflective Teaching*
Vivien Hodgson *et al*: *Beyond Distance Teaching, Towards Open Learning*
Peter Linklater: *Education and the World of Work*
Graeme Moodie: *Standards and Criteria in Higher Education*
John Pratt and Suzanne Silverman: *Responding to Constraint*
John T. E. Richardson *et al*: *Student Learning*
Derek Robbins: *The Rise of Independent Study*
Alan Woodley *et al*: *Choosing to Learn*
Gordon Taylor *et al*: *Literacy by Degrees*
Tight: *Academic Freedom and Responsibility*

The Crisis in Higher Education

Competence, Delight and the Common Good

Marjorie Reeves

The Society for Research into Higher Education
& Open University Press

Published by SRHE and
Open University Press
Open University Educational Enterprises Limited
12 Cofferidge Close
Stony Stratford
Milton Keynes MK11 1BY

and
242 Cherry Street
Philadelphia, PA 19106, USA

First Published 1988

British Library Cataloguing in Publication Data

Reeves, Marjorie
   The crisis in higher education: competence,
   delight and the common good.
   1. Higher education. Philosophical
   perspectives
   I. Title
   378'.001

ISBN 0-335-09530-5

Library of Congress Cataloging-in-Publication Data

Reeves, Marjorie.
   The crisis in higher education: competence,
   delight, and common good/Marjorie Reeves.
   p. cm.
   Bibliography: p.
   Includes index.
   ISBN 0-335-09530-5
   1. Education, Higher – Great Britain – Aims and objectives.
   2. Education, Higher – Economic aspects – Great Britain.
   I. Title
   LA637.R44   1988
   378.41 – dc 19   88-22467 CIP

Typeset by Rowland Phototypesetting Limited
Bury St Edmunds, Suffolk
Printed in Great Britain by St Edmundsbury Press Limited
Bury St Edmunds, Suffolk

Contents

Acknowledgements

The genesis of this book lies in the discussions which the Higher Education Group has held over a number of years into questions of values in higher education. This group which came into being as a result of Sir Walter Moberly's book, *The Crisis in the University* (1949), met as the University Teachers' Group until widening its scope with the expanding situation in higher education. Over the years the themes of its discussions have been markers of the changes in climate of opinion and focal concerns. To some extent this book reflects these shifting emphases. Its great debt is to the many informal exchanges of ideas which have sparked off the mind and to the tough arguments which have clarified issues. It is only possible here to name a few of the many in whose debt I stand. Professor Stephen Prickett, Dr. Stephen Medcalf, Dr. Anthony Nuttall, Dr. Kathleen Bliss, Dr. Geoffrey Price, Dr. Desmond Ryan are among those from whom I have drawn much – though they would probably not agree on many points with my thinking. Professor W. R. Niblett and Fr. Peter Cornwell read the book and encouraged publication, as did Professor Duncan Forrester. Dr. Sinclair Goodlad not only read it but helped greatly in advising on publication. The conversations which flow through this book are in part a record of the past decade, but the hope is that such searchings of values will continue with vitality and serious purpose.

Marjorie Reeves,
St. Anne's College,
Oxford.

1

Education for Use and Education for Delight

I was a little stranger which at my entrance into the world
was saluted and surrounded with innumerable joys
                                        Thomas Traherne

To be human is to be part of a society of explorers.
                                        Michael Polanyi

Education is about exploration and therefore about relationships. A small child exploring his world experiences relationships both soft and hard: contact with his mother can be satisfying and soft; contact with the door-knob can be resistant and hard. The drive to explore expresses two needs. To get what he wants a child struggles to overcome obstacles and master techniques, such as how to manipulate the door-knob and get through the door. But when he has burst through he is delighted and fascinated by this strange new world, for the drive to master the means can have been actuated by an urge of pure curiosity – to discover what lay beyond that door barrier. That simple early experience encapsulates at least part of the meaning of education: the experiences of power and delight mingle. On the one hand, there is the drive to master skills and techniques which give power to use, power to manipulate, power to gain control *over* something – and in that preposition *over* is contained the sum of Man's technological relationship to the world. On the other hand, constantly welling up, come the feelings of delight and wonder at the intricacy, fascination or sheer beauty of what has been discovered. The interaction of these two types of experience can most easily be seen in the exploration of the natural world, or the world of things. But exploring and establishing contact with people can be equally a power game or an experience of delight which, in this case, is best described as 'communion'. People can be used and people can be enjoyed. But here it also becomes clear that use and delight can become deadly enemies of each other, though not necessarily so.

Today knowledge for use holds the centre of the field. Politicians and economists say that to keep up in the technological race we must reap a proper return from investment in education in terms of people equipped to use their skills and knowledge in practical ways. Moreover, the young want the knowledge which will furnish them with a paper qualification to open desirable career-doors. And indeed the mass of the next generation need a multiplicity of skills – far beyond the three Rs. – to cope with their lives. Power to cope is the minimum which everyone needs; power to add to our technological expertise as a nation is the maximum expected of Higher Education. Some would add: anything further is a luxury which we cannot afford. Thus the key question in a series of Government pronouncements has been: how (is) the educational regime connected with the labour market and the imperatives of job creation?

'Above all', says the White Paper, *Higher Education: Meeting the Challenge* (April, 1987), 'there is an urgent need, in the interests of the nation as a whole and therefore of universities, polytechnics and colleges themselves for higher education to take increasing account of the economic requirements of the country. This aim . . . must be vigorously pursued.' This represents a major shift of attitude towards higher education. 'This is the first time in history that universities have been associated with the training of "agents" for the creation of wealth,'[1] observed one Vice-Chancellor as long ago as 1979, and his words are echoed by a recent commentator: 'the White Paper . . . completely reversed the accepted philosophy that higher education benefits the individual, which in turn benefits society.'[2] It is only fair, however, to point out that this official shift was preceded by a movement of serious educational thinking in which the needs of individuals to adjust to social demands were stressed as much as the requirements of society itself.

In 1980 a group of distinguished people published a manifesto headed 'Education for Capability', republished with minor amendments in 1981 and 1982. The 1981 version states:

that there is a serious imbalance in Britain today in the full process which is described by the two words 'education' and 'training'. Thus, the idea of the 'educated man' is that of a scholarly, leisured individual who has been neither educated nor trained to exercise useful skills. Those who study in secondary schools or higher education increasingly specialize; and normally in a way which means that they are taught to practise only the skills of scholarship and science; to understand but not to act. They gain knowledge of a particular area of study, but not ways of thinking and working which are appropriate for use outside the education system.

We believe that this imbalance is harmful to individuals, to industry and to society. Individual satisfaction stems from doing a job well through the exercise of personal capability. Acquisition of this capability is inhibited by the present system of education which stresses the importance of analysis, criticism and the acquisition of knowledge and generally neglects the formulation and solution of problems, doing, making and organizing; in fact, constructive and creative activity of all sorts.

The resolution of this problem in Britain has been vitiated by discussing it in terms of two cultures: the arts and the sciences. It is significant that we have no word for the culture that the Germans describe as 'Technik' or the mode of working that the French describe as a 'Métier'.

We consider that there exists in its own right a culture which is concerned with doing, making and organizing. This culture emphasizes craftsmanship and the making of useful artefacts; the design, manufacture and marketing of goods and services; specialist occupation with an active mode of work; the creative arts; and the day to day management of affairs.

We believe that education should spend more time in teaching people skills and preparing them for life outside the education system; and that the country would benefit significantly in economic terms from this re-balancing towards education for capability.

One practical outcome of this manifesto was the establishment of a Royal Society of Arts Recognition Scheme to encourage initiative in promoting an education that 'gives due regard to competence, to coping, to creativity and to co-operation with others, for the art of living requires the development to act wisely rather than to pursue knowledge for its own sake'.[3] The 1982 advertisement of this scheme described its aim as 'to identify, encourage and publicize educational programmes designed to help people . . . to learn to live and work more effectively'.[4]

Many of these statements ring bells of assent, (for example, the present writer remembers producing an article in the 1940s entitled 'The Culture of the Job'). Many perceptive points are made. But the more one examines its basis, the more clear it becomes that, though the diagnosis of symptoms in terms of the present imbalance may be right, the nature of the disease is wrongly understood. This concept of education deliberately attempts to create a dichotomy between the scholar who is taught to understand but not to act; between the activities of analysis, criticism and acquisition of knowledge on the one hand, and those of problem solving, doing, making, organizing, constructing and creating on the other; between 'pursuing knowledge for its own sake' and learning to act wisely and live effectively. Stated thus the promoters of education for capability might perhaps agree that such a sharp dichotomy is not true to the way life is lived. Scholars act and create; analytical skills are continually used in problem-solving and 'doing'; 'knowledge for its own sake' can teach wisdom. The juxtapositions set out in their manifesto are entirely comprehensible in terms of the 'serious imbalance' which rightly worried its promoters so much, but their dichotomies are false ones.

In the ongoing debate it is instructive to note one or two of the many reactions to the pressure for 'usefulness' in education. In 1985 a Green Paper on 'The Development of Higher Education into the 1990's high-lighted the growing sense of a long-term danger that the 'imbalance' feared by the promoters of 'capability' was now tipping the other way. A *Times* leader (23/5/85) stigmatized it as 'noticeably one-track. The track is sign-posted in the Green Paper's opening statement: "It is vital for our higher education to contribute more effectively to the improvement of the performance of the economy".' Even in its own terms the Green Paper was seen to take too short-term a view in 'the facility with which it equates economically relevant with technological and vocational'. Two reactions in *Times* articles, whilst expressing considerable sympathy with the Government's worries about educational failures, both pointed up the confusion in the educational thinking of the Green Paper. Roger Scruton (12/6/85) wrote: 'It argues, reasonably enough, that education should be funded by the public only if it benefits the public. But its utilitarian idea of benefit, suggesting that there might be an economic standard of academic success is riddled with confusion.' He then developed his argument on the true relationship between education and the community:

> Prosperity is not an end but a means. . . . We should not value education as a means to prosperity, but prosperity as a means to education. Only then will our priorities be right. For education, unlike prosperity, is an end in itself. . . . Of course, education is also profitable. But if you fix your eyes too firmly on the profit, you lose sight of the thing itself. . . . The profit of education persists only so long as you don't pursue it. Furthermore, the profit comes to us by an 'invisible hand'. Economic planning is no more likely to succeed in this field than in any other. . . . In this area wise planning means the careful avoidance of plans. . . . And education should provide not the narrow details of tomorrow's technology (which will soon be yesterday's) but the intelligent discipline which adapts itself to new and changing circumstances precisely because it is attached to none. Higher education, in short, must be pointless and irrelevant. Otherwise it has no value.

David Watt's reaction to the Green Paper was to reach for his copy of Newman's *Idea of the University* and set Newman's eloquent and liberal view against this 'bleak accountant's view of higher education, as a kind of servicing industry which needs to pull up its socks and pay its way'. He accused the Government of turning its back on Newman in a fit of anti-intellectual revulsion. But, he asked, 'where is the Government's justification for burning down the house in order to cure a little rising damp?'[5] He made the telling point that nothing will be achieved in education without the cooperation of intellectuals: 'the Government may dislike or despise them but it cannot hope to educate if it makes no effort to understand and compromise with them . . . The fact (is) that their priorities include a love of truth for its own sake and a belief that it is, in Enoch Powell's word, "barbarism" to attempt to evaluate higher education in terms of economic performance'. This was a political statement, underlining the fact that politicians, if they wish to be successful, must take into account the basic motivation of the groups they wish to influence or persuade. It was all the more significant that, in making such a statement, Watt ended by preaching to Mrs Thatcher in terms of what he calls 'Newman's tremendous peroration'.

Now, in 1988, institutions of higher education find themselves pitchforked into 'this new environment of the market-place'[6] by the provisions of the Education Bill. The new system of contracts through which public funding will be distributed is aimed 'to strengthen the commitment of institutions to the delivery of the educational services'[7] which it is agreed with the funding body they are to provide. In the words of one Vice Chancellor 'all this sounds like the language of a rather tough purchaser who is hoping in due course to cut down on the amount of buying that he has to do.'[8] Market values appear to be overwhelming education. Of course such a statement as Scruton's provocative pronouncement that it is of its essence that higher education should be pointless and irrelevant is deliberately one-sided. But equally so is 'the achievement of greater commercial and industrial relevance,'[9] as the major goal in higher education. We come back to the meaning of education for the person. The school of thought which makes competence in the market place the top priority envisages only half a person. It sees the tool-maker and the user; it seeks the organization of knowledge for purposes beyond itself; it stresses the connections between 'knowing' and 'doing' – 'doing' seen in terms of social usefulness. All these aspects are vital to the life of individuals and communities today. But they embody only half a truth about human-beings. Curiosity – in Einstein's words the 'holy desire of curiosity' – is a universal human urge, though – alas – too soon quenched for many by fear and starvation, or under-nourishment, both physical and spiritual, or the sheer limitation of a dreary environment. It is a mistake to dismiss curiosity, or the desire to find out, as simply the whim or prerogative of a small intellectual élite who batten on the rest of the community in order to till 'for its own sake' some obscure field of knowledge which is useless in community terms and therefore seen as a piece of self-indulgent selfishness.

If we go back to our small children in primary school we can already see two motivations in operation. In 1985 The Royal Society of Arts gave an award to a group of Infant School children for their entrepreneurial enterprise in designing and marketing mugs – and the emphasis was not on the designs they had created but on the profit they had made. Their faces (in a newspaper photograph) showed the excitement and satisfaction of achievement. Here successful entrepreneurship in our society was equated with grasping an opportunity which yielded material profits. Yet we have only to look around in a lively primary school to observe how equally satisfying is the drive to explore for its own sake and with what exuberance and delight the quest is pursued. Matthew, aged eight, cannot yet read, but his passion is moths and he can 'read' the pictures in the *Oxford Book of Moths* to identify 'the one I found on my bed last night'. Giles is suddenly 'hooked' by the medieval village and – to the relief of his mother – abandons bicycle technology to spend an absorbed weekend manufacturing an 'old document' with Domesday entries. And, of course, it is not only children who are captured by the enchantment of discovering an external reality. This is the driving force of all great thinkers and scientists and one could cite innumerable examples. To give only one, Eve Curie vividly portrays the fascination, obsession and passionate love which carried her mother through years of incredible labour until she had isolated radium in pure form. On the evening of her victory, so Eve relates, she and her husband stole down to the shed which was her laboratory: '(they) stood looking at the radium, glowing blue in the dark. "Look. Look!", whispered Marie Curie like a child'.[10]

Putting aside the, as then quite unsuspected usefulness of such a discovery, we must ask: What is the significance of such a personal drive? What is the point of such knowledge? If we do not wish to give it the separate existence or 'sake' of the classical academic justification ('knowledge for its own sake'), we must find some way of describing what is undoubtedly a satisfying personal experience. The 'person' is enriched by a relationship which may not immediately be turned to any practical end at all. In some mysterious way he is captured by some 'thing', some figure in the past or some idea. Without getting entrapped in the difficult question of whether this 'something' can really take the initiative, we can use such language figuratively in saying that it is *as if* the 'it' puts out a feeler or hook, or *as if* 'it' speaks first. What is clear is that the person responds spontaneously to a sense of intrinsic worth in something outside himself. As Iris Murdoch has said: 'The direction of attention is, contrary to nature, outward away from self which reduces all to a false unity, towards the great surprising variety of the world and the ability so to direct attention is love'.[11] The fascinating and mysterious aspect of this mood is that a person is committed to this sense of worth before he really knows much about the subject of his investigation. His response is excitement, perhaps wonder, certainly desire to know more. Wonder and delight are uniting emotions, not separating ones. In plunging into the kind of enthusiasm I have been describing, we relate ourselves imaginatively to that which we are setting out to explore, in a certain sense we 'hold communion with it'. At a later stage of exploration we shall probably use the separating techniques of analysis freely, but in the first instance it is a vision in wholeness that we see – a kind of instant recognition.

I have stressed this apparent dualism between 'use' and 'delight' because these two concepts seem to be in collision at this time. But, of course, in the process of learning they interact in many subtle ways. Furthermore, while both these factors are of primary importance as what we may call the sparking-off mechanisms, growing through learning is obviously a far broader process which has to meet some of the deepest needs of human beings. In a later chapter we will examine some of these specific needs which we ought to be meeting through the provision of educational experiences.

It is significant that in the present climate, with its obsessive concentration on things, people should be turning back to Martin Buber whose thought exercised so strong an educational influence between the two World Wars. In the little book *I and Thou* he starts from two 'primary words', both combined words spelling out relationships. One is the combination I-Thou; the other the combination I-It. 'The primary word I-Thou can only be spoken with the whole being. The primary word I-It can never be spoken with the whole being.'[12] In an I-Thou experience we open ourselves wholly to another 'reality' with the intention of knowing, not using. This is the complete relationship in which the full being of a person is realized through attention to the not-self. 'The Thou meets me. I step into direct relation with it. . . . I become through my relation to the Thou; as I become, I say Thou. All real living is meeting.'[13] These relationships can change. Buber makes it clear that a 'Thou' can become an 'It' and vice versa. But the thrust of his thinking challenges sharply our present obsession with the *It* relationships, with the tool situations that control so much of our lives. Spontaneous, outgoing delight withers in so far as we reduce our world to a collection of useful 'its'. In particular Buber is warning us against allowing the obsession with 'use' to take over education. To all of us he might be saying: There will be no lack of tool experiences in modern education but for heaven's sake try to orchestrate the moments of 'real meeting' when the young are enabled to step right outside themselves, caught up in the fascination of encounter. These are the moments of richest growth for a person.

The accusation of selfishness is, however, a serious one. Words like 'enjoyment', 'delight', at once evoke an image of the individual who hugs his secret treasure to himself in solitude. 'So much of schooling constitutes a process of systematized selfishness', says Alec Dickson, arguing for service to the community as a method of study in higher education.[14] David Brockington, in the same symposium, speaks of 'self-centred personal satisfaction in specialized knowledge not usually applied to the world outside of the education system itself' as the generally approved justification of education.[15] Those who press home the case for useful knowledge are, in many cases, reacting understandably against an extreme individualism which recognizes no duty or obligation in scholarship. Yet they caricature the real driving force of true scholarship. The argument of this book is that all learning is 'under authority' or under obligation. The first authority is that of the outside reality to which the person responds. I shall argue in the last chapter that the basis of this authority is ultimately theological. The compelling motive in putting oneself under this authority is not to gain personal fulfilment or personal pleasure but to give glory (or love) to reality. Personal enrichment is the by-product of this process, the unsolicited gift of reality. It is 'an act committed to the conviction that there is something there to be discovered. It is personal in the sense of involving the personality of him who holds it . . . but there is no trace of self-indulgence. The discoverer is filled with a compelling sense of responsibility for the pursuit of a hidden truth which demands his services in revealing it.[16]

But the process can turn bad unless an interlocking imperative is recognized – that of sharing riches. In terms of the old legend we were told as children, the one who travels guarding his fire in his bosom without using it to guide others finds it extinct at the end of his journey, whereas he who carries it aloft as a beacon to all finds it blazing more brightly at the end. Enthusiasm has somehow to be shared. Again we go back to the Primary School and find children catching us by the hand to come and see what they have been making. Exploration must find its outlet in a work of creation *which can be shared*. It may be a child's gorgeous riot of colour, or his model castle, or it may be a scholar's work of synthesis. In a wide spectrum of people's creative acts we recognize two common qualities: first, the 'work' is a subtle fusion of materials used (paint, wood, clay, words, symbols or whatever) and personal feeling or thought; secondly, the 'work' is to be shared, it is a form of communication between persons. The artist or scholar who hides or destroys his work is an aberration. Obviously some works have a much narrower range of communication than others, but all human works are meant to 'speak' to someone. Alfred Whitehead said: 'Unapplied knowledge is knowledge short of its meaning'. A more satisfactory statement would be: 'unshared knowledge is knowledge short of its meaning'.

The concepts of making and doing cannot be confined too narrowly to the making of useful artefacts or deeds of practical service. A piece of writing can be a true 'making' if its creator speaks to others out of personal understanding and imagination. The word 'use', again, can have two aspects: the straightforward one of using knowledge to solve problems in the ordinary business of living, and the uses of enthusiasm or the creative 'word' to lift and enrich this business of living to a liberating level. Knowledge for use and knowledge for delight should not be set in opposition: they are obverse and reverse of one coin. In another *Times* article (28/10/85) Anne Sofer made a strong plea to overcome their disjunction:

> It is the recurring British phenomenon of polarization that is the root of the problem. People feel obliged to align themselves with opposing camps. They must subscribe either to the view that education is to do with personal development and fulfilment of potential (hence maximum individual choice unrelated to national need) or to the view that the purpose of education is to meet the needs of the economy (and hence greater national direction). . . . A synthesis is desperately needed: at the very least an acceptance that the development of the individual and the needs of the economy must be held in balance.

2

The Tyranny of Pre-packaged Information and the Concept of Personal Knowledge

Our knowledge and our being are related

Michael Polanyi

Instead of offering an 'open world' of nature and of man to be explored and experienced, education has been allowed to 'set' in a series of moulds labelled curriculum and syllabus. This has happened through the slow shaping of inherited knowledge and skills into traditional forms – a process which in Western culture has gone on over many centuries. But we should note that these traditions which now govern, to a large extent, the education of all were formed in the matrix of special education for the few. Bernard Shaw's reputed quip 'My education was interrupted by my schooling' serves to point up the truism that the young grow through the total experience of their environment which goes on for twenty-four hours of the day. Impressions pour in, feeding personal understanding and forming social habits. What goes on outside is often a more powerful education than the selected experiences in an educational institution. In fact there have always been two forms of education running side by side: community education, gained as a growing member of a society where skills, know-how, knowledge for survival, have always been picked up 'on the job' with the minimum of books or theory, and specialized education in which some have been withdrawn from common experience to receive bookish and theoretical education related to specific functions in society. For Western cultures this second type of education has its roots in the early middle ages when the so-called 'barbarian' peoples who took over Western Europe, aspiring to emulate the Greek and Roman culture they admired, patronized monastic institutions and schools where the remnants of classical education were salvaged and the basic curriculum of *Trivium* (grammar, logic, rhetoric) and *Quadrivium* (arithmetic, geometry, astronomy, music) was gradually evolved. What is fascinating to observe is that, in a world where – so it would seem to modern man – technological education was the pressing need, the highest value was placed on the skills of communication and the theory of number. Later, as the medieval university developed out of ecclesiastical beginnings in the twelfth and thirteenth centuries, the emphasis was still theoretical, on the study of philosophy and theology, law and medicine. Law was treated, not in terms of the practical fisticuffs of the Common Law courts, but as the study of Roman Law, while medicine, based on the ancient Greek textbooks, was far removed from the needs of plague-stricken communities or the messy surgery of the battlefields.

Community education for the masses, however, went on all the time, unnoticed and undervalued. The history of attempts from the sixteenth century onwards to provide educational institutions specifically oriented towards the new scientific and technological needs of society is significant for its record of failure to make any real impact on the tradition of bookish learning which in England survived the Reformation with very little change. The consistent undervaluing of apprenticeship as a form of education reveals how little the hidden benefits of practical community education were realized and when, in the nineteenth century, the pressing need for universal education was at last grasped, it was to a watered-down version of the traditional book-learning of the élite that the reformers turned. The basic skills of the three Rs. were, of course, seen as necessities, but beyond these the school-teachers and inspectors turned instinctively to bits and pieces of the body of knowledge accepted as 'our culture' – to geographical and historical facts such as names of capitals and counties and dates of the kings of England, to tabloid information on great authors, and to 'object lessons' which inculcated a few facts about the natural world. As schooling for all was extended, more and more of a child's time and attention was withdrawn from the experience of discovery in the community world and focused on the narrow world within the school four walls, where skills were learnt without relation to situations in which they would be tested and knowledge was presented in bundles of facts which had little purpose except to satisfy the inspector.

Of course there was another side to all this. The passionate campaigners for universal schooling saw themselves as rescuing children from cruel exploitation by a conspiracy of hard-faced employers and greedy or desperate parents. How far, far better to sit in rows and learn poetry than sit down a mine shaft and cry in the dark! 'Community education' had never been the idyllic growth in relationships which some of the pictures of primitive life painted, for instance, by Margaret Mead, tended to convey, while the dark satanic mills of industrialization threw into dramatic relief the vulnerability of the young. All the same, something important was lost when education became synonomous with schooling and, more particularly, when that schooling was modelled almost wholly on the book learning of the élite.

Matthew Arnold constitutes a prophetic case-study in the malaise about a universal bookish education which in his day had hardly yet begun to be felt but which we recognize only too well today. The interesting point is that his reaction against 'bookishness' was partly the result of his revulsion against so much of what he saw as he inspected elementary schools, and partly the expression of a much more complicated dissatisfaction with his own higher education and development as a poet and as a man of letters. Here was a man steeped in the classics, an avid reader in many fields, a leader in culture, who suffered acutely because he could not resolve all 'meanings' in an inward harmony. In his poem

'Empedocles on Etna' (1850), Arnold cries out against the load of external knowledge which oppresses the spirit:[1]

> We scrutinize the dates
> Of long past human things,
> The bounds of effaced states,
> The lines of deceased kings;
> We search out dead men's words and works of dead men's hands;
>
> We shut our eyes and muse
> How our own minds are made,
> What springs of thought they use
> How rightened, how betrayed –
> And spend our wit to name what most employ unnamed.
>
> And still, as we proceed
> The mass swells more and more
> Of volumes yet to read,
> Of secrets yet to explore,
> Our hair grows grey, our eyes are dimmed, our heart is tamed.

In the words of Honan, Arnold's latest biographer, Empedocles was 'victimized by whole libraries', by 'a vast multitude of facts awaiting and inviting comprehension'. He quotes Arnold's cry: 'Congestion of the brain is what we suffer from . . . I . . . cry for air, like my own Empedocles'.[2]

In his famous essay 'Culture and Anarchy' Arnold finally clarified his deep unease about the dilemma of learning in modern society. Mere bookishness he dismisses as inadequate and he cannot even put his trust in higher culture, except as defined in a particular sense. His definition of true culture speaks to our condition today:[3]

> a pursuit of our total perfection by means of getting to know, on all matters which most concern us, the best that has been thought and said in the world; and through this knowledge turning a stream of fresh and free thought upon our stock notions and habits.

'Matters which most concern us' and 'a stream of fresh and free thought upon our stock notions' – there are the hall-marks of the 'personal knowledge' for which we are groping today. And Arnold's identification of the three enemies of true culture is also prophetic: first, the mechanical and material civilization which imperils 'inwardness of spirit'; secondly, our competitiveness which separates us from our fellows; thirdly, our over-specialization and absorbtion in one particular pursuit.[4] What we need is inward living to set us imaginatively free, sympathetic sharing in the development of others and a harmonious expansion of powers unfettered by the bars of specialization. Arnold's passionate feeling for 'inwardness' applied as much to children in state schools as to the élite in higher education. In a little work written for schools in 1871 he cries out against his impotence to break the tyranny of the external word:[5]

For one who believes in the civilizing power of letters and often talks of this belief – to think that he has for more than twenty years got his living by inspecting schools for the people, has gone in and out among them, has seen that the power of letters never reaches them at all and that the whole study of letters is thereby discredited and its power called in question, and yet has attempted nothing to remedy this state of things, cannot but be vexing and disquieting . . . 'We have not wrought any deliverance in the earth'.

Arnold's, of course, was a very one-sided view: he did not recognize the power of science. Nevertheless, his 'power of letters' is still an elusive magic which we seek as it still evades us. The advocates of 'Capability', however, think rather in terms of the tyranny of letters and make plans to break it. Is the inherited knowledge in books magic or tyranny? Clearly, for some, in all periods, books have spelt magic and if we recall, more specifically, those who were beneficiaries in the earlier part of this century of the newly accessible secondary and university education, we must conclude that their eagerness to learn was not entirely motivated by career ambitions. The new horses, when led to the springs of learning were, on the whole willing, even eager, to drink. The 'power of letters' was shown to be more than the treasure belonging to a small privileged élite. True, it was mostly the lower middle classes who trod the newly opened avenues to learning and perhaps most manual workers have seldom felt that they had a share in a bookish cultural heritage. Yet the power of curiosity and the power of letters were never wholly class-bound. The astonishing range of scientific and literary pursuits catered for in the famous educational institutions for working men and the avidity with which members pursued learning for its own sake as well as for use bear witness to a drive to know which is a universal human trait. In nineteenth-century Coventry, for instance, there were seven 'Mutual Improvement Societies' in which members exchanged information on their different hobbies. Joseph Gutteridge, who belonged to one of these, formed his own natural history museum and gave talks on such subjects as 'The Physiology of the Digestion'.

Yet today the magic has largely faded. There can be little doubt that many of the present generation of all classes are aware chiefly of the tyranny of learning. This is the situation which has prompted the Capability Movement. The argument here is that we need to identify immediate causes and to seek specific remedies rather than promote a drastic revolution in educational philosophy. Why are so many young people alienated from their studies? It was in the 1960s that teachers began to worry about motivation in pupils. The fact that this was the period of expansion suggests one fairly superficial reason. Ironically, the very great gain made in establishing the rights of all to schooling up to 18, and beyond for many, carried its own dangers. Notoriously, established rights tend to be undervalued and the fact that secondary, and to a certain extent higher education, could now be taken for granted reduced the need for personal commitment. Students began to speak gloomily of themselves as passive packages on the conveyor belt. Passing from a period of expansion to one of reduction has drastically altered the situation but has done nothing to revive enthusiasm for learning. The causes of disillusionment, however, go much deeper. One surely lies in the hardening of arteries that has taken place in the corpus of learning, perhaps as a direct result of the widening of education opportunity. For the concomitant to this has been the growth of a universal examination system.

The written examination which tests knowledge of a particular package of information is a modern invention. It was the universal character of secondary and higher education that produced the demand for a standardized classification of students in terms of a common currency of paper qualifications. But standardized examinations can only be based on agreed and delimited areas of study (subjects) and defined packages of information (syllabuses). The essence of a modern examination system lies in the carving up of the corpus into 'limbs' and 'joints' which become dead when detached from the organic whole. Furthermore, the method of examining puts a heavy emphasis on the reproduction of factual information, since this alone can be confidently assessed in quantifiable terms. A primary response in wholeness cannot in itself be measured. You cannot set as an examination question: 'Enjoy this poem'. You can only test the secondary, analytical stage: 'Give three reasons why you enjoy this poem'. Gallant efforts are made by examination boards to introduce questions or exercises to test thought, powers of reasoning, judgement, feeling, but – in the humanities at least – the examining exercise all too often drifts back to the model factual answer which can be taught – and in teaching it we lose sight of the truth which C. S. Lewis, writing of 'Eng. Lit.' test-papers, put so clearly:[6]

> Everyone now laughs at the old test-paper with its context questions. . . . 'What good can that sort of thing do a boy?' But surely to demand that the test-paper should do the boy good is like demanding that a thermometer should heat a room. It was the reading of the text which was supposed to do the boy good; you set the paper to find out if he had read it.

Practical pressures from employers, parents and the community at large keep this system going. But there are academic reasons also. Most academics believe that subjects have their own inherent structures and can only be properly studied by a series of logical steps in learning and understanding. The very use of the word 'discipline' underlines the notion of an objective requirement to which submission must be made. This is an academic conviction which is hard to challenge because it has so much scholarly integrity and experience behind it. And it seems indisputable that learners of certain skills for example, in languages, mathematics, philosophy, must put themselves 'under obedience' to the rules of that discipline. But, while techniques must be learnt in a certain order, the content of knowledge is another matter. In history, for instance, there are certain desiderata – getting a clear chronological sequence of events or a horizontal grasp of happenings contemporary with each other are examples – but is it necessary to acquire this framework in a set order of 'outlines' or

'periods'? More generally, is there really a body of historical facts which
'everyone ought to know'? The bottom falls out of this argument when we
observe that people soon forget what was externally learnt for examination
purposes: the package is simply thrown away when no longer needed. It is time
to challenge conventional academic structures of knowledge, just as it is time to
question the value of the traditional examination system. Both can become
tyrannies.

Even so, we are not yet at the bottom of the problem of alienation from
inherited learning. Is it not part of the turning away from the values and
life-style of this present society? Disbelief, scepticism, cynicism about the
purposes for which the people around them live are redirected back on to their
teachers and on to the book culture which supposedly shaped them. 'They are
all liars and hypocrites', says the student in a low, expressionless voice, as if
repeating a lesson, but he lets out a string of abusive terms in a vivid range of
language. 'They are all lead-dogs of capitalism', shouts the politically-oriented
student. Extreme and distorted views – yes, but a milder degree of cynicism is
wide-spread. Reluctantly, students may recognize that some of their teachers
are dedicated to their subjects, but so many of them do not believe that these
senators have been taught or can convey anything approaching the wisdom
which they are seeking.

Yet inspiration does come to students, but comes so often 'on the side'. A
student conference, searching for the New Jerusalem, arranges an evening of
readings on the literature of Utopias, ranging from medieval dreamers and
prophets to modern poets. Under the guidance of a sympathetic don the factual
background to each writer is carefully sketched in, the readings are delivered
with genuine feeling and there is no doubt about the involvement of the
audience. It is a serious, moving occasion, with the unspoken thought behind it:
this is part of the heritage from the past which we treasure and from which our
imaginations take nourishment. One feels, almost palpably, that a relationship
has been established: the theme itself is linked with thoughts and aspirations
about present living. These dreams and prophecies come alive because in a
particular sense they are 'relevant'. Does it follow that knowledge of the past
only becomes relevant when it can be consciously linked with our human
predicament today? For some this is certainly the way to light up the imagination, but it gives too narrow a meaning to the word 'relevance'. The ways in
which people light up through relating themselves to some remote and
apparently irrelevant theme from the past are mysterious. Equally so is the
fascination for some particular phenomenon in the natural world which catches
others. What we may call 'personal relevance' seems to be a key factor but an
unpredictable one calling for further examination.

The sharp contrast between the pre-packaged information of the syllabuses
and 'real' knowledge can only be understood through the factor of personal
commitment. We have already touched on this as the mysterious hidden
element in all education. Desire to know, we reiterate, springs not only from
desire to use but also from the explorer's instinct. And this is where the
strangeness lies, for, as we have said, the exploring mind commits itself

imaginatively to the belief that there is something 'out there' which is worth knowing *before* there can be any exact grasp of what that 'worth' is. What is felt is the excitement or passion associated with an intuition of impending discovery: 'an act of heuristic conjecture (is) a passionate pouring of oneself into untried forms of existence.'[7] Commitment to a sense of worth forms a relationship in which the hard discipline of learning can be sustained precisely because there *is* a relationship.

A century ago John Henry Newman analysed this commitment in his *Grammar of Assent*. He contrasted 'real' assent with notional assent or inference. 'Real' assent is unconditional, one and indivisible. 'An act of assent, it seems, is the most perfect and highest of its kind when it is exercised on propositions which are apprehended as experiences and images, that is, which stand for things.'[8] By 'things' Newman appears to mean independent realities, for he contrasts propositions as 'notions' with propositions as 'realities'. 'An act of inference which is the most perfect and highest of its kind (is) exercised on propositions which are apprehended as notions, that is, which are creations of the mind.'[9] On the other hand the unconditional commitment of an act of real assent rests entirely on belief in the objective reality of the 'thing': 'An act of assent rests wholly on the thesis as its object and the reality of the thesis is almost a condition of its unconditionality.'[10] Experience, mediated through the imagination, supplies these 'objects': 'In its notional assents as well as in its inferences, the mind contemplates its own creations instead of the impressions they have left on the imagination.'[11] Newman's words 'real assent' portray the outgoing act of a whole person, responding through the imagination to a reality which demands commitment before a process of analytical understanding can begin.

In our own day Michael Polanyi has become the exponent of a similar belief in what he calls 'personal knowledge'. He was convinced that the dominant philosophy of 'scientific objectivity' was leading men along a false trail, that man was essentially a discoverer and that discovery, the source of all knowledge, sprang out of personal response to reality. The process of knowing does not begin with collecting facts but with observing an odd 'fact' (or facts) which has not yet been seen as significant but may be and which puzzles or intrigues the observing person, even to the point of obsession: 'the personal skill of seeing which facts are significant is an integral part of discovery'.[12] And this personal response to 'intimations of reality'[13] must be with passion: 'Any process of enquiry unguided by intellectual passions would inevitably spread out into a desert of trivialities. Our vision of reality, to which our sense of scientific beauty responds, must suggest to us the kind of questions that it should be reasonable and interesting to explore'.[14] Beforehand, the whole process appears vague and indeterminate:

> It starts with the solitary intimations of a problem, of bits and pieces here and there which seem to offer clues to something hidden. They look like fragments of a yet unknown coherent whole. This tentative vision must turn into a personal obsession, for a problem that does not worry us is no

problem . . . This obsession, which spurs and guides us, is about something that no one can tell; its content is indefinable, indeterminate, strictly
personal. Indeed the process by which it will be brought to light will be
acknowledged as a discovery precisely because it could not have been
achieved by any persistence in applying explicit rules to given facts. The
true discoverer will be acclaimed for the daring feat of his imagination,
which crossed uncharted seas of possible thought.[15]

Thus Polanyi takes his stand on the conviction that 'this personal intuitive
"intellectual love"' is the heart of science.[16] Summing up this position, he
declares: 'I have tried to demonstrate that into every act of knowing there enters
a tacit and passionate contribution of the person knowing what is being known,
and that this coefficient is no mere imperfection, but a necessary component of
all knowledge.'[17]

Where Polanyi's insight is apt to shock the academic lies in his constantly
reiterated claim that the process of knowing *starts* with belief – belief in a reality
as yet only dimly perceived but apprehended in its 'worthness'. This is where he
breaks out of the sterile objective/subjective disjunction. The process of knowing cannot be 'scientifically objective' in the sense of an impersonal, distanced
collecting of data, nor should it be understood as subjective, in the sense of an *I*
seeking to draw in and impose its own meaning on fragments of evidence from
outside. It is neither of these but rather the explorer–person 'meeting' a reality
which is 'true, out there, universal and binding'[18] and which he believes to be
worthy of exploration in its own right: 'All life is a heuristic enterprise, invoking
at every stage the search for new coherences, solutions, for new problems . . .
The method is always one of attending *from* the known *to* the unknown.'[19]
Discovery implies belief in the existence of an objective truth. In the structure of
knowing, objects of knowing are reflected which are independent and claim the
allegiance of the knower. Discovery is a successful contact with a hitherto
hidden reality, where 'real' can be defined as 'that which is expected to reveal
itself indeterminately in the future'. Confidence is based on commitment to this
reality: 'the fiduciary passions which induce a confident utterance about the
facts are *personal*, because they submit to the facts as universally valid. . . .
According to the logic of commitment, truth is something that can be thought of
only by believing it'.[20] Here Polanyi illumines the true meaning of that classic
phrase 'Knowledge for its own sake' which academics can use with such
passionate conviction but which is a red rag to so many bulls who can be
appropriately represented by the Spaniard Miguel de Unamuno in his utterance: 'Knowledge for the sake of knowledge, truth for truth's sake, this is
inhuman.'[21] Of course the phrase as it stands is misleading: the true affirmation
is 'Knowledge for the sake of the objective reality which carries worth for the
seeker.' And the excitement which fuels the explorer's commitment stems from
his belief in this reality as capable of unsuspected self-revelation:[22]

> This capacity of a thing to reveal itself in unexpected ways in the future I
> attribute to the fact that the thing observed is an aspect of a reality
> possessing a significance that is not exhausted by our conception of a

single aspect of it. To trust that a thing we know is real is, in this sense, to feel that it has the independence and power for manifesting itself in yet unthought ways in the future.

Polanyi was writing out of the experience of an original scientist but he has bequeathed to us an extraordinarily illuminating concept for understanding the inner processes of education. He would have perceived the students' predicament of today when required to learn a series of discrete facts which constitute no problem and arouse no intellectual passion. The student crisis of meaning finds Polanyian expression: 'The mind strives in the whole range of personal being', 'to achieve integration and understanding.'[23] He was on the verge of giving us a gospel for students. All true learning is meeting ('All real life is meeting'[24]): it can be disturbing, conflicting, stretching, but it is personal. There is always, however, an implied risk. Drusilla Scott glosses Polanyi thus: 'Commitment is to reality and may require a comprehensive conversion, or only a small change in our interpretative framework. It involves risk: we may be mistaken, but we have to "take these chances in the hope that the universe is sufficiently intelligible to justify this undertaking".'[25]

Here the educationalist has to ask: What are the sources of that vitality which enables a learner to be venturesome and commit himself to such risks? There is a paradox here, for the risk-taker as explorer is so often he who starts out from a secure base. This has often been pointed out in the case of explorers in the physical world, but Polanyi makes an important point about the springs of exploring vitality in the intellectual realm. He distinguishes between *tacit* and *explicit* knowledge. Tacit knowledge is a *given* interpretative framework, partly inherited, as developed by a society over many years, and partly acquired. Explicit knowledge comes through attending focally to something. The point that Polanyi then makes is that tacit knowledge must precede explicit knowledge. The process of education is one of developing 'the conceptual powers to recognize things familiar and things novel and to fit them into one's own framework of tacit knowledge'. All discovery starts from a given base of tacit knowledge and Polanyi stresses the importance of an 'intellectual dwelling-place', this is, the cultural traditions and values which people 'in-dwell' as their mental habitat and which are relied on as they move out to fresh discoveries. 'All pursuit of truth requires an initial in-dwelling of the traditions of one's culture . . . All human beings learn and grow in the acritical framework of their own culture'.[26] For all men Polanyi desires a happy dwelling place of the mind, for no one can set out on discovery from a vacuum. Polanyi was really enunciating two fundamental educational aims: to provide for each mind its 'happy dwelling place'; to set each person's feet on the path of life as a way of discovery. His critique of present education centres largely on the failure of teachers to carry out the first aim adequately. The present emphasis on developing rationality tends to turn out teachers 'who lack both the inclination and the resources to furnish their pupils' minds with the tacit content so essential for the building up of a foundation and conceptual framework on which to rely . . . In this kind of situation the discovery method is unlikely to succeed . . . the pupil lacks the happy dwelling place of the mind which should serve to guide his explorations'.[27]

It is striking that Iris Murdoch, in her examination of the 'sovereign good', like Polanyi, warns against the false subjectivity in which the *I* is at the centre of the circle: '. . . real things can be looked at and loved without being seized and used, without being appropriated into the greedy organism of the self'.[28] Her concept of attention as a 'patient loving regard which is an obedience'[29] is the intrinsically personal attitude required in all true 'knowing'. It is deeply personal; it is not subjective. For the activity of attending takes us clean out of ourselves; it also puts us 'under authority'. Couched in the highest terms of the 'sovereign idea', Murdoch declares that this 'cannot be taped – it is in its nature that we cannot get it taped. It always lies beyond and it is from this beyond that it exercises its authority'.[30]

Both Polanyi and Murdoch present a challenge to education, and to higher education in particular. But before we consider it in practical terms, two other points must be emphasized. First, it is of the essence of the exploring relationship that the explorer takes what he finds into himself, assimilating the new knowledge to the old and adding to or modifying his world picture accordingly. The simile which comes to mind is that of taking a new piece of furniture into the interior dwelling place of the personality, shifting the other pieces around to accommodate the new, perhaps throwing a bit out or altering the colour scheme to achieve a new harmony. The important thing is that the new piece is not left outside the house, or even in the passage. Personal knowledge effects transformations. Whether discovery is in the world of nature or of man, it modifies or even radically changes a person's world picture. Learning which does not transform is not education at all. The second point is that the true explorer's house is never exclusive. There is always a great coming and going. Polanyi points out that no two people inhabit the same thought world. Nonetheless, our search for truth must not be for private possession but for communication. It must be 'with universal intent', says Polanyi.[31] In his search for truth man attempts to satisfy his standards and needs (admittedly self-set) by finding what can be seen and shared with others. 'In order to be satisfied, our intellectual passions must find response.'[32] Personal knowledge needs to authenticate itself through communication, and Polanyi speaks of the 'conviviality' of such sharing.

What guidance, then, have these educational insights to give us? We have spoken of the intellectual homelessness of many students today. Some, finding the vacuum intolerable, incarcerate themselves in false homes which are ideological fortresses or prisons. The rest wander in the wilderness. We may, perhaps, be sceptical of Polanyi's faith in traditional culture as still providing a credible home.[33] For many students it now seems too ruined to give shelter. In a paper given to the Higher Education Group Brian Cox discusses the accusation that the teaching of literature, for instance, bolsters up tradition and an unchanging view of society by the 'passivity and quietism' of its usual methods.[34] Against this he cites Lionel Trilling's assertion of the aggressive character of real literature, asking us terrifying personal questions and transforming lives. It is through disturbing experiences rather than anodyne modes of learning that students will begin to construct a home again. Hence the first essential now in the humanities is to start building a new house, with old materials, maybe, but designed with a new sensitivity and awareness of the emotional blockages which have caused such general alienation. Above all, students themselves must participate in designing and building the new house.

How do we set learners in secondary and higher education back on to the path of discovery which they have lost? Can the pre-packaged system of education be changed? Can these dry bones live? It was the breath of the Lord which gave the answer to Ezekiel's question and it may be chiefly the breath of imagination working within the system which will be needed to resurrect the exploring spirits. There is a challenge here that must be met by the kind of 'aggressiveness' that Trilling was talking about, that is, by presenting our subject matter as that which disturbs, challenges, even, in some sense, invades – for only so does it become 'relevant'. This is certainly true for the humanities and social sciences. The 'aggression' can be located both in the sharp question or observation designed to penetrate and in the disturbing 'word' of the text itself under consideration. So a student can be provoked into action – the action of asking questions and seeking answers. At its best this can expand into a personal learning project. The word project has become popular and cheapened, but in its essence it encapsulates the whole concept of 'personal knowledge' or the process of building a cultural home of one's own. It starts with identifying a problem or a question. This should be one which has 'hooked' the student already, but it will be defined and modified through a process of interchange between teacher and student. This stage embodies the process of moving from the known base outwards towards the unknown. Informational background and necessary skills form the discipline of obedience which becomes acceptable as personal involvement in the topic grows. The actual work of research, investigation, experiment (according to the nature of the subject) should bring this commitment to a high pitch in the excitement of discovery and the activity of relating the new to the existing framework of ideas. Finally, solutions take shape and something new is created – a presentation of 'objective' evidence, certainly, but 'created' because shaped by a particular person. And personal creations, as we have said, must be communicated in some form or another to other persons.

Of course this is an ideal sketch. The problem may prove a non-starter or too unmanageable; the student's commitment may fail; his intellectual limitations may frustrate him. But those of us who have examined 'long essays' in the humanities catch the note of personal commitment all the time among both weak and strong students, and realize that even the weak can carry away something permanent from this type of work. In practical terms they have (to a varying extent) learnt to define problems, cope with techniques of investigation, marshal evidence and construct arguments. In terms of the imagination, they have related themselves to a piece of past experience which becomes part of and enriches their own. A similar assessment of gains could surely be made in the case of scientific projects. This discussion of projects has been couched in individual terms but an almost more important step – because a greater break with tradition – is the encouragement of cooperative projects in which individual assessments take place within the context of team-work. Academics are obsessed by the necessity of assessing individual performance, but in the world at large qualities of team-work have as high a valuation. Arnold's identification of 'our competitiveness which separates us from our fellows' as one of the enemies of authentic culture rings very true today. A drastic modification of ideas on examinations is needed.

Written examinations are the chief lion in the path. Granted for the moment that we cannot alter the public demand for paper qualifications and therefore we must live with this concept of examinations, the needs of persons demand that we seek a radical change in the values enshrined in examination testing. In the first place, more weight should be given to asking candidates to identify important questions and problems rather than requiring them to give neat, buttoned-up answers. This can be done by various kinds of open-ended questions, for example, asking the student to set his own question and, in answering it, to explain why this is to him an important question. Secondly, in the humanities at least, the transforming power of the imagination, fusing information with 'personal knowledge', can be given scope even in the tabloid form of three-hour examination answers. Thus a student can be asked to reflect on a piece of past experience (literary or historic) in the light of a comment on our present human predicament. There are also possibilities for inviting artistic approaches to literary/historical subjects, such as the scenario for a play or opera, a poem or a sketch or cartoon. Thirdly, General Papers on the course, specifically set to test thought and judgement, are important, though often vigorously opposed by examiners as a trap for the unwary – as indeed they can be. Fourthly, much more weight in the total assessment of students should be given to project work, cooperative as well as individual. Admittedly all this is likely to make examining more problematic, more subjective and more time-consuming. It is a price we have to pay, for we shall not resolve our present crisis of culture until we break the tyranny of examining dead information by finding ways of evaluating those more elusive qualities alongside the limited range of intellectual competence for which the system is designed.

But, assuming for a moment that we can brush aside this examination mosquito, we must see that the real 'end' of all personal knowledge is a 'doing'. A 'doing' in this context is a two-way process. It is, in the first place, the act of embodying the excitement of discovery in personal terms which convey meaning to other persons. It begins with an act of 'focal awareness' which is 'that kind of integrated, unselfconscious, ongoing attention which we experience when we are fully engaged in some skilled, creative action.'[35] It is a creative act in so far as something new is interpreted in the imagination, translated into a form which assimilates new experience to old, and expressed in a medium which speaks aloud. This is what Brian Cox, in the paper quoted above, calls 'writing as action'. But, secondly, the very act of 'doing' illumines understanding, for the struggle to communicate meaning clearly and fully brings its own reward in enriching and refining the truth within us. We actually need relationships calling for 'speech' in order to know the meanings inside ourselves. That 'speech', that 'doing' can of course take many shapes and use many media. Here we must reiterate that the notion of 'doing something' must not be limited to craftsmanship or practical service, important as these are. Words are materials which can be shaped to creative purposes every bit as much as clay, wood or paint. Writing need not always remain in the debased servitude of the examination answer. The essential point, in whatever form the 'doing' takes, is the fundamental need to share enthusiasm, to communicate what has become of 'worth' to the discoverer. If personal commitment to learning becomes in itself a kind of relationship, it is equally true, as Polanyi says, that this leads to an outgoing desire to relate one's own 'thought world' to other people's. There are so many obvious ways of doing this but one – which is of great significance today – might not be thought of in this context. It is the idea of Study Service on which recent studies have been made. In various programmes students relate themselves and their learning to people in the community and their specific needs. Again, this is a two-way educational process of illuminating one's own learning by sharing it with others. We shall return to this theme later.

The language of banqueting seems the natural language for the sharing of good things. Plato used it. Dante used it. Now Polanyi has turned to it in his concept of 'conviviality', the sharing of the good things of mind and spirit.[36] To apply such language to most students' experience in higher education may evoke the wry thought that the only conviviality they find academically is champagne-drinking to celebrate escape at the end of examinations. So much for formal education. But we have only to look around to see where real conviviality – in Polanyi's sense – is to be found among young people of all kinds today: in spontaneously organized music, drama and dance groups, in pop groups, in exhibitions of their own modern art, in the 'do your own thing' one meets in the foyer of the National Theatre, in collectors' clubs of every variety, in absorbing discussions on topics in which they feel really involved, in shared action for causes about which they feel passionately. Even protest marches and demonstrations have their 'convivial' aspect (more important, perhaps, than the demonstrators realize). There is no lack of 'personal knowledge' to be shared in festive ways. But too often it has little to do with their official education. Contemplating the student scene, we see also that other lot, the crowd of aimless wanderers with no enthusiasm or passion to celebrate anything. On the one hand, enthusiasm, marginalized, is poured out on the side; on the other hand, vitality seems to be smothered. This is a state of affairs we ought not to tolerate but it cannot be remedied without a fundamental shift in attitudes in the relevant authorities, in short, a removal of both market demands and subject requirements to supporting positions instead of primary ones on the educational stage, in order to give space to the student himself in the centre of the stage, playing out the drama of his personal development, limited and bounded though this must be by those supporting factors.

3

The Use and Abuse of Analysis in Education

And still dividing and dividing still . . .
                                        Wordsworth

We desperately need to work for synthesis as a corrective to
the exaggerated bias towards analysis
                                        J. V. Taylor

'Knowing' through analysis can be broadly distinguished from 'knowing' through apprehension in wholeness, though both may be intertwined in the same process. That we cannot get on without analytical methods of thought is demonstrated by the previous sentence. At every stage of attaining understanding we distinguish, categorize, define and place in juxtaposition. Equally, at every stage of scientific investigation dissection seems the paramount method. Perhaps in the process of building up knowledge the 'learned knife' has been the most useful tool of the human mind. It is tempting – but perhaps unprofitable – to digress on to speculation about its origins. What we should note is that, deriving inspiration from classical models, medieval thinkers set us on the road to abstract analysis. Their higher curriculum began with a training in using the tools of intellectual analysis, their lecture form in the *Quaestio* was one of dividing and subdividing the problem and its possible answers, their encyclopedias were compendia of information neatly categorized and pigeon-holed, and their highest attainment was the *Summa* which ordered all knowledge in clear divisions. But this type of intellectual analysis remained confined within a narrow framework: words and their uses, the existing stock of knowledge about the world, philosophical and theological concepts to interpret this – these materials were arranged and rearranged endlessly. Only a few tried to break out and to acquire new knowledge by direct observation and experiment. The plant of knowledge became pot-bound.

The scientific revolution of the sixteenth and seventeenth centuries broke the pot in its drive to understand the physical universe but accompanying this drive the instinct to break down into constituent parts remained and this became the dominant mode of exploring the universe. It is easy to over-dramatize this development: the method of understanding concepts by pulling them apart was already well-established. But the spectacular growth of analytical observation and categorization came at a time when men were asserting in a new way their power to question and master their world. If the concept of Renaissance Man has been overplayed, yet when Galileo declared that nature was to be grasped by measurement, not sympathy, he was expressing a new attitude,[1] while in the writings of Francis Bacon we hear the proclamation of a new role for man in his right to question and master his world. Bacon categorically claimed the Adam-right to dominate and use the natural order: 'Only let the human race recover that right over nature which belongs to it by divine bequest'.[2] A man should 'endeavour to establish and extend the power and dominion of the human race itself over the universe'[3] and this drive should be directed towards practical benefits. 'Truth and utility are here the very same things, for human knowledge and human power meet in one. . . . Now the empire of man over things depends wholly on the arts and sciences. . . . The true and lawful goal of the sciences is none other than this: that human life be endowed with new discoveries and powers.'[4] 'So', declared Bacon, 'among all the benefits that could be conferred upon mankind, I found none so great as the discovery of new arts, endowments and commodities for the bettering of man's life. . . . If a man could succeed . . . in kindling a light in nature . . . that man would be the benefactor indeed of the human race, the champion of liberty, the conqueror and subduer of necessities'.[5]

Thus Bacon tied the acquisition of fresh knowledge to its use and he saw the sovereign method as that of observation and analysis. He envisaged a vast programme of data-collecting, making a great heap of particulars which would then be sorted into categories, classified and organized for use. But such a marriage between science and technology could clearly not be carried out in the ancient universities, still set in their medieval mould. Bacon was not the only prophet who pressed for a new kind of institution in the late sixteenth and early seventeenth centuries. Sir Humphrey Gilbert urged Queen Elizabeth to establish a special academy 'To try owt the secrets of nature' and present to the government 'all those their proufes and trialles'.[6] Sir Francis Kynaston had plans for the education of a new type of élite in the 1630s[7] and Samuel Hartlib in 1647 wanted to replace professorship in Divinity, Civil Law and Rhetoric at Gresham's College in London by chairs of technology. In the mid-seventeenth-century new social trends – a progressive and wealthy merchant class, a Puritan clergy of energetic mind, an economy ripe for technological progress – encouraged new educational ideas. Thus the left-wing Puritan, Gerard Winstanley, wanted everyone to be educated 'in every Trade, Art and Science whereby they may find out the Secrets of the Creation' and 'know how to govern the Earth in right order'.

These schemes were all abortive. Although some higher education in scientific and technical subjects, geared to the new mercantile class, was carried on in the eighteenth-century Nonconformist schools and academies, no new ideas touched the ancient universities. The Royal Society could not find a congenial home in either Oxford or Cambridge and carried on its investigations outside the university framework. But the scientific method was still advancing to conquest, and now among philosophers in the cultural fields. Spinoza had declared: 'From now on we are to observe and describe man and his works as if there were but lines, planes and bodies'.[8] The assumption developed that 'to know' was to analyse, quantify and organize in measurable categories. Bacon had already declared his mistrust of the imaginative approach to learning as distorting or discolouring the nature of things: 'The understanding must not be supplied with wings but rather hung with weights, to keep it from leaping and flying'.[9] Voltaire praised Locke, who wanted to abolish figurative language as misleading, for applying the principles of dissection to human psychology.[10] Auguste Comte pronounced the final verdict of Positivism on the necessity of bringing every human activity under the imperium of the scientific method: 'We shall find that there is no chance of order and agreement but in subjecting social phenomena, like all others, to invariable natural laws . . . in other words introducing . . . the same positive spirit which has regenerated every other branch of human speculation'.[11]

The all-powerful alliance of a dominating scientific mode of thought and method with a technology on the move really begins in the nineteenth century with the new technical institutions and the rise of the civic universities. But this relentless march was not without challengers in the name of imagination and poetry. The first was William Blake, with his outcry against the fetters which he believed the new sciences were riveting on the human mind:

> For Bacon and Newton, sheath'd in dismal steel, their terrors hang
> Like iron scourges over Albion. Reasonings like vast Serpents
> Enfold around my limbs, bruising my minute articulations.
> I turn my eyes to the Schools and Universities of Europe,
> And there behold the Loom of Locke, whose Woof rages dire,
> Wash'd by the water-wheels of Newton; black the cloth
> In heavy wreath folds over every Nation: cruel Works
> Of many wheels I view, wheel without wheel, with cogs tyrannic,
> Moving by compulsion each other; not as those in Eden which,
> Wheel within wheel, in freedom revolve, in harmony and peace.
>   ('Jerusalem', 15, 6–20)

In Blake's poetry Urizen stands for the 'single vision' which limits, divides, separates, as in his illustration where Urizen is reaching down with giant calipers to measure off space. Under his baneful influence the senses shrink and grow opaque, the eye of man narrows, the self grows small. Blake castigates the scientists:

> You accumulate Particulars and murder by analysing, that you
> May take the aggregate, and you call the aggregate Moral Law.

For Blake inspiration, enthusiasm and imagination are the trinity that must expose the Spectre of false Reason and 'single vision':

> I come in Self-annihilation and the grandeur of Inspiration;
> To cast off Rational Demonstration by Faith in the Saviour,
> To cast off the rotten rags of Memory by Inspiration,
> To cast off Bacon, Locke and Newton from Albion's covering,

To take off his filthy garments and clothe him with Imagination;
To cast aside from Poetry all that is not Inspiration . . .
To cast off the idiot Questioner, who is always questioning,
And never capable of answering . . .
Who publishes Doubt and calls it Knowledge; whose Science is Despair.
                                                                    (Milton, 42, 34 ff.)

Wordsworth's protest against scientific culture stemmed from the priority he gave in education to a sense of 'presence', that communion or conversation with the 'speaking face of earth' which he felt so vividly throughout his own growing up.[12] Experience, he saw, came *before* analysing, 'presence' before systematizing. Only when the imagination has been kindled and nourished can reason rightly begin to order and classify what has been experienced. In words which foreshadow Arnold's, he attacks the bookish education of the model child:

He knows the policies of foreign lands;
Can string you names of districts, cities, towns,
The whole world over, . . .
                    he sifts, he weighs;
All things are put to question . . .
                    ('The Prelude', V. 319–23)

The fundamental truth which Wordsworth proclaimed was that primary knowledge is delight:

For knowledge is delight; and such delight
Breeds love; yet, suited as it rather is
To thought and to the climbing intellect,
It teaches less to love than to adore;
If that be not indeed the highest love!
                    ('The Excursion', 346–50)

Without this imaginative experience science is only pseudo-knowledge:

. . . that false secondary power by which
In weakness we multiply distinctions, then
Deem our petty boundaries are things
That we perceive and not that we have made.
                    ('The Prelude', II, 216–19)

But, given a primary relationship in delight and wonder, science can become inspired:[13]

. . . a precious visitant . . . worthy of her name
For then her heart shall kindle, her dull eye,
Dull and inanimate, no more shall hang
Chained to the object in brute slavery.

Finally, in 'The Excursion' Wordsworth launched his great attack on the analytical approach to knowledge:

. . . Shall men for whom our age
Unbaffled powers of vision hath prepared
To explore the world without and world within,
Be joyless as the blind? Ambitious spirits –
Whom earth at this late season hath produced
To regulate the moving spheres and weigh
The planets in the hollow of their hand;
And they who rather dive than soar, whose pains
Have solved the elements, or analysed
The thinking principle – shall they in fact
Prove a degraded Race? . . .
go, demand
Of mighty Nature, if 'twas ever meant
That we should pry far off, yet be unraised;
That we should pore, and dwindle as we pore,
Viewing all objects unremittingly
In disconnection dead and spiritless;
And still dividing, and dividing still,
Break down all grandeur, still unsatisfied
With the perverse attempt, while littleness
May yet become more little; waging thus
An impious warfare with the very life
Of our own souls!

('The Excursion', iv, 944–68)

Shelley joined in the attack when, in his *Defence of Poetry*, he denounced the corrupting power of the tool-mentality:[14]

> The cultivation of those sciences which have enlarged the limits of the empire of man over the external world has, for want of the poetical faculty, proportionally circumscribed those of the internal world; and man, having enslaved the elements, remains himself a slave.

Hence:[15]

> The cultivation of poetry is never more to be desired than at periods when, from an excess of selfish, calculating principles, the accumulation of the materials of external life exceed the quality of the power of assimilating them to the internal laws of human nature.

So the early Romantics in England – and there were Continental voices, such as Goethe's, in tune with theirs – fought the rising empire of science and technology. They lost their battle as far as education was concerned. They tried to defend a qualitative approach to knowledge against a measuring, numbering scientific approach which alienated Man, they believed, from the creation. They tried to substitute an organic concept of science for a mechanistic one – hence their enthusiasm for biology. They wanted to preserve the relationship between men and their environment, opening the whole personality towards the reality of the 'other' rather than allowing the intellect alone to advance in assault upon it – with its knife. But they could not stay the advance. From the sixteenth to the nineteenth century the new scientific method conquered in realm after realm. To know was to analyse into parts. The parts must come before the whole. It was probably of great importance that there was always a dialectical debate proceeding, on the one hand, with the Platonic belief in the prior reality of 'wholes', and, on the other, with the Romantic instinct for participation in and communication with the natural world. Through most of this period the voices of protest and prophecy cried out and alternative ways of knowing through experience fed the imagination and fostered perception through the senses. But nothing could stay the progress of scientific method as it ripped through the subjects and captured the educational processes. In 1754 the Society for the Encouragement of Arts, Manufactories and Commerce in Great Britain was formed and, as the Society of Arts, it pushed forward technical developments by stimulating projects in every branch of applied science and technical education, as it is still doing today. In 1799 the Royal Institution was created 'to teach the application of science to the common purposes of life'.[16] Humphrey Davy, who was associated with it, clearly expressed the technological purpose of Man when he wrote: 'by his experiments to interrogate nature with power, not simply as a scholar, passive and seeking only to understand her operations, but rather as a master, active with his instruments'.[17] By the nineteenth century the pressure of industrial expansion was turning voluntary experiment into official institutions. University College, the seed of London University, was founded in 1826, while the history of civic universities outside London begins in earnest with the foundation of Owens College in Manchester in 1851. From this point the development of scientific and technological education has gone steadily forward through a whole range of institutions. True, most of these have been mixed in their aims and the courses they have offered, but it could be said that the general thrust of expansion in higher education has been towards 'interrogating nature with power'.

Where do we stand now in the great debate between the artist and the scientist/technologist? Of course the Romantics were unfair. They only saw a sinister conspiracy against the imagination. We must correct the balance in four ways: first, there is the enormous value to mankind of the material achievements of science and technology and the importance of continuing to extend this 'mastery'; secondly, the practical and psychological needs of the young demand 'knowledge for use'; thirdly, in the very realms where imaginative delight holds sway analysis is an essential tool of communication; fourthly, many great scientific thinkers testify to the intermingling of the imaginative and intuitive, on the one hand, with the observational and analytical, on the other.

On the first point there is little need to elaborate. *Pace* Shelley, material advance *does* matter and the great conquests of the scientific–technological cohorts can be seen as wonderful gifts to mankind, even though acknowledged as highly dangerous. The advocates of training for practical utility argue convincingly that for survival in any sort of peace the human race must step up the work of harnessing natural resources to human needs and therefore that the next generation must be trained as useful and wealth-producing members of society. We would add, also as good stewards of exhaustible resources.

The second point is crucial to the argument here. Each generation needs to be equipped by its education with the competence to cope with daily life, with the 'tools' in general use to support that competence, with some notion of how to tackle problems and with some experience in cooperative enterprise. In a rapidly changing world training to adapt is constantly needed. All this is common-place among educational statements, but we still do not fulfill these purposes very successfully. The psychological need to be recognized as competent, capable of doing a job, acknowledged by adults as 'useful', is of paramount importance. Recognition of capability has two facets: the obvious one is the pay packet, and the tragedy of today's muddled society is that this is denied to so many young people. 'Worth' measured in hard cash must never be under-estimated as a factor in the making of a person. But there is also the more subtle recognition in terms of social usefulness, of the 'real' contribution a young person makes to the community in which he/she is embedded. This must be seen in wider terms than paid employment. A whole series of responsible or 'capability' relationships needs to be built up. All this forms part of the secure base which the young need before they can adventure out with confidence. Polanyi spoke of the intellectual base, but a social base from which to move is almost prior. It is centred in the value which family, school and community place on an individual's services, his 'doings' in society. We shall return to this need in a later chapter.

Thirdly, analysis provides the tool of clear 'language' and this is important at all levels for meaningful discourse and cultural transmission. The learning of a language which has progressed beyond grunts is an education which at once places the human young in a special category. Throughout history this linguistic energy has been a mysterious factor. It has been directed towards clarifying, differentiating and organizing experience which would otherwise remain chaotic and uncommunicable. Learning 'language' (including non-verbal languages) can therefore be a liberating experience, creating the means of bringing order into experience and of sharing it. Unless we learn to insert the knife into an undifferentiated collection of impressions, unless we have the language to classify them, unless we have the concepts within which to order the whole, not only does thought remain inchoate and feeble, but imagination cannot reach its full wing-span. The joy of clarification alone is an immense mental stimulus: to dispel mists, to put sharp lines where blurred ones were, to lay bare concealed contradictions and juxtapose opposites gives, not only increased mastery over material, but also a sense of freedom to move with some confidence in the midst of confusions. Moreover, to return once more to Polanyi, he points out that tools need not be handled as external objects: 'We pour ourselves out into them and assimilate them as part of our own existence.'[18] The methods of Socrates is a shining example of how, by dissecting concepts, young men might be led towards an understanding which expressed response in wholeness. His searching dismemberment of language was not designed to murder faith but to resurrect it in clearer shape. It is often argued that the conquests of a scientific and analytical method in the literary field have been a disaster, that one cannot understand great works of the imagination by processes of quantifying and separating, but this is not wholly true. Morton Bloomfield, a distinguished literary historian, defends analysis thus:[19]

> The experience of a work of art, if it is a successful one, is no doubt unified, but if appreciation is to progress beyond mere experience, intellectual distinctions must be made. Intellectual distinctions are intellectual and they exist for the purpose of comprehension. Criticism, if it is to be more than a recall of feeling, is an intellectual discipline and necessarily involves the use of intellectual categories such as form and content. *We must not mistake the categories for the thing itself; they are created to enable us to understand it.* . . . Even if form and content are indissolubly united in a great work of art, it is still worthwhile in our comprehension of it to separate them. (My italics)

As Collingwood once said of statistics, analysis is a good tool but a bad master. And this is true, not only for scholars, but for the young generally who need to refine their means of communication.

Fourthly, the divide between the artist and the scientist is becoming blurred as the psychological factors in the process of discovery and the relativity of the scientist's position *vis-à-vis* his 'object' are investigated. The imaginative leap proposing a hypothesis and the intuitive grasp of an answer before the slow work of experiment and analysis is finished, reveal the scientist as an artist. Arthur Koestler produces many examples of this in *The Act of Creation*. Thus Karl Friedrich Gauss wrote:[20]

> At last two days ago I succeeded, not by dint of painful effort but so to speak by the grace of God. As a sudden flash of light, the enigma was solved. . . . For my part I am unable to name the nature of the thread which connected what I previously knew with that which made my success possible.

Koestler points out that 'in the popular imagination these men of science appear as sober ice-cold logicians, electronic brains mounted on dry sticks. But if one were shown an anthology of typical extracts from their letters and auto-biographies with no names mentioned, and then asked to guess the professions the likeliest answer would be: a bunch of poets or musicians of a rather romantically naive kind'. He cites Max Planck's statement that the pioneer scientist must have 'a vivid intuitive imagination, for new ideas are not generated by deduction but by artistically creative imagination'.[21] Einstein went to the heart of the matter: 'I maintain that cosmic religiousness is the strongest and most noble driving force of scientific research. . . . What a deep belief in the intelligence of Creation and what longing for understanding . . . must have flourished in Kepler and Newton, enabling them as lonely men to unravel over years of work the mechanism of celestial mechanics . . . It is cosmic religiousness that bestows such strength.'[22]

Yet when all this is said, the analytical method of the sciences which now pervades almost every subject in the educational curriculum has swung the balance too heavily one way. 'Divide and Rule' is an approach to mastery but not necessarily to delight. Cutting up subject-matter makes manageable packages but hardly contributes to 'personal knowledge'. 'We must not mistake the category for the thing' warns Bloomfield. 'We murder to dissect', said Wordsworth. 'An unbridled lucidity can destroy our understanding of complex matters', says Polanyi.[23] Experience ought to precede analysis, yet so often the knife is applied before the student has had time for real apprehension in wholeness, 'breaking down all grandeur'. If language is to provide a liberating experience, the young must be free to use it, not only as the precise tool of clear thinking, but to articulate 'meanings' in whatever strange, chaotic style they need to unstop the springs of imagination and give utterance. William Blake gives us a brilliant juxtaposition of the two languages:[24]

> When the Sun rises, do you not see a round disk of fire, somewhat like a Guinea?' O no, no, I see an innumerable company of the heavenly host crying "Holy, Holy, Holy, is the Lord God Almighty".'

'Literature is concerned with the power of the icon and the image', says David Martin.[25] All students need such a study to nourish and enrich their own self-expression by widening their range of symbols, as, for instance, in discovering the great biblical and classical worlds of symbolism. Such language has a resonance of its own. In the symposium on Utopias, referred to earlier, one could feel the reverberations of the literary symbols echoing all round the room. In contrast we can set the words of Louis Dupré: 'The flattening of language empties the word of its sacred power. . . . Words no longer intrinsically mean: they serve a function within an arbitrary, limited system of expression. Obviously, such a highly restricted use of language severely limits the scope of experience: we think and feel within the possibilities offered by language.'[26]

Concepts without percepts are empty. The concept seeks to encompass the whole of the phenomenon and it reaches its goal by way of classification, subsumption and subordination. Already in the eighteenth century Berkeley had given the warning: 'Whenever we proceed from percept to concept we find ourselves under the tyranny of words'.[27] Language ought to be pegged to experience, we have said, yet we hurry on in education to the analysing and abstracting stage, thus interposing a grey barrier between learners and the rich world to be experienced. This was already seen by Schiller:[28]

> We know that the sensibility of the psyche depends for its intensity upon the liveliness, for its scope upon the richness, of the imagination. The preponderance of the analytical faculty must, however, deprive the imagination of its energy and warmth. . . . impressions can move the soul only as they remain whole . . .

And Stuart Hampshire today echoes him: 'The price of full rationality is a separation of argument and of systematic understanding from the primary emotions'.[29] The endless web of words in which we analyse and abstract can become the funeral pall for emotional vitality. So we see the impoverishment of language in educational writing. It is academically more respectable to say something impersonally than directly, and so, for instance, writers of history text books develop an almost unconscious habit of turning all statements into an abstracted form. As the influence of a dehydrated style spreads, the young find it increasingly difficult to find an adequate language in which to express personal experience. Where there are no overtones of symbolic meaning words express only 'the monotones of life' and, argues Theodore Roszak, the main result of the analytical approach to knowledge has been 'to drive all meaning into monotonous linguistic formulations'.[30] This is a kind of shrinkage (flattening in Dupré's words) or reductionism in language whose purpose is to master and control, 'to have it under your hand'. But language should also express relationships. Books should be not just words, but people speaking. In an essay 'On reading books from a half-alien culture' Stephen Medcalf asks:[31]

> . . . what is it to be a person? Are we atomic individuals, independent substances only externally related, communicating by constructions and works of art placed between us? In that case, reading a book is like contemplating an artefact designed to elicit such and such responses in the reader, and if the artefact does not work we legitimately adjust it. Or are we beings who exist partly in terms of each other, capable of and needing radical empathy, so that our languages, even over a gap of time, are relations partly internal to ourselves, intuitively understood? In that case, reading a book is entering the truth of someone else's mind, and, if we cannot enter, it is we ourselves who must change.

Certainly the language of great books has power to change, sometimes sharply. 'A book', said Kafka, 'must be an ice-axe to break the sea frozen within us'.[32] How little 'edge' do text-book abstractions retain!

Along with abstraction goes fragmentation. Ordering means separating and pigeon-holing – the very expression 'pigeon-hole' embodies the notion of boxed-in separateness. The intimate relationships which fundamentally connect every aspect of knowledge to every other, like a seamless robe, are quickly torn apart to make learning more manageable. The standard lecture is organized in headings and sub-headings and its success in 'getting the stuff over' is measured by the ease of note-taking. The lecturer who suddenly sees side connections as he talks and so wanders off into fascinating by-ways is usually written off as a bad lecturer. A famous scholar in Oxford, of the old school, who was notorious for this, habitually reduced his audience to two or three who, nevertheless, remained enthralled by his erudition and wit on unexpected and irrelevant topics. Liam Hudson saw the assumption behind the way he was taught as the belief that all knowledge consisted of 'facts', hard little nuggets of information like separate building blocks.[33] This objectified relationship underlies much academic teaching. If our attitude is really one of assembling and manipulating nuggets of information, we communicate this view of knowledge as an inert collection of separate pieces to our students. Yet there is for many of us a prior attitude towards our subject, one of relating ourselves to it as something of worth which evokes excitement, perhaps wonder, to which we are committed and which we wish to communicate. The trouble is that we so seldom reveal this fundamental attitude. There is such pressure to get on with the analytical process that we rush straight into the second stage of learning, without pausing for contemplation or reflection. We habitually deal with pieces before wholes. Yet there are great exceptions among teachers, those with imaginative powers who – often unaware of what they are doing – create a vision, a presence, a real 'something', before they begin to analyse it. Equally at the other end of the learning process, we allow too little time for realizing in the imagination what we have taken to bits and reassembled mechanically, according to given rules. We hurry on to the next topic without giving time for contemplating the intrinsic qualities which have been revealed – of intricate beauty and order, maybe, or of tragedy or heroism. We have taught *how* the subject works, but not what it *is* in relation to the human knower. So the manifold, complex and rich shapes of knowledge are pressed into hard little nugget-moulds.

The total effect of too much analysis is for many students a disastrous experience of alienation from their academic studies. The form in which these are presented interposes a barrier between themselves and the world to be experienced, instead of opening doors into discovery. The language currency alienates from living reality by imposing the grey tyranny of fragmented experience reassembled in the dead shapes of abstract concepts. The demand for instant dissection destroys the moment of wonder or delight. Everything shrinks, ourselves included. In Wordsworth's phrase: '(we) dwindle as we pore, viewing all objects unremittingly, / In disconnection dead and spiritless'. There is no place for contemplation of the whole and no time to relate one's own world of thought and feeling to the new knowledge. The resonance of great symbols dies away in the flat tones of the textbook. The academic world becomes a dead world, a wilderness of inanimate things from which the living person escapes with relief into his own world of personal dialogue.

Yet vision can change the whole landscape and the dead can live again. If the vision is there, the analysing and ordering of experience enhances comprehension. A poet may teach us here. Dante modelled his youthful love poetry on troubadour song, but when he wanted to display his learning he tried to philosophize his *canzone* in the *Convivio*. He planned eleven books but he never got further than the fourth, for poetic understanding did not marry well with philosophical dissection. He really began to get a clue to the meaning of the universe and of himself when he left his half-built house of abstractions to wander in the 'dark wood' of his own confusing experience. Thence began his poetic journey towards the true meaning of things. The *Divina Commedia* conveys its meanings in a succession of magnificent images, yet it is the most intellectual of poems. Experience is categorized and ordered within a tight framework of number symbolism and correspondences, and when Dante finally attains the ultimate vision of the Godhead it is in the abstract geometric image of three interlaced circles that he embodies the mystery of the Trinity:

> In the profound and shining being of the deep
>   light appeared to me three circles, of three
>   colours and one magnitude;
> One by the second as Iris by Iris
>   seemed reflected and the third seemed afire
>   breathed equally from one and from the other.
>   (*Paradiso*, XXXIII, 11. 115–20)

So at the end of his life Dante could blend the languages of art and of science in a creation to which philosophical and theological analysis give an edge, but which is suffused by a light of multiple depths and meanings. The vision fades, but it leaves him whole and integrated as a person:

> To the high fantasy here power failed;
>   But already my desire and will were rolled,
>   even as a wheel that moveth equally, by
> The love that moves the sun and other stars.
>   (*Paradiso*, XXXIII, 11. 142–5)

It is, perhaps, fanciful to find the union of the two methods symbolized in the vision of the New Jerusalem at the end of the Apocalypse (Rev. 21, 22). St. John is overwhelmed with wonder but the Angel takes a rod and *measures* the City. It stands solidly foursquare in its symbolic mathematics, but within it 'the leaves of the Tree are for the healing of the nations' (Rev. 22, 2). We do not abandon the framework provided by the quantifying and dissecting exercises, but it must enclose a living experience.

4

Student Needs

A human-being is an inhabitant of a world composed, not of
things, but of meanings

Michael Oakeshott

Man is a creator of meanings

William Bouwsma

Needs and Wants: are they the same thing? To a teacher observing student
behaviour the answer would often seem an emphatic *No*. And from the State too
– for different reasons – we seem to be hearing a strong negative: the 'wants' of
individuals must be moulded into conformity with the 'needs' of the technological community. So, by a process of socialization, individual aspirations must
be 'managed', to fit in to the system. Yet Thomas Traherne wrote: 'You should
want like gods'.[1] Gods are not noted for conformity. In contrast to the prevailing
official attitude, let us affirm that the most important aim in higher education is
to enable students to become 'godlike' in their wants. But what does this mean?
On one interpretation it has more than a sniff of the superman. In much more
naive terms the completely individualistic 'want' was earnestly expressed by an
American student who said: 'My purpose in college is to round out my
personality by broadening my background'.

   Yet it was, I believe, the extreme emphasis on individualism which was
ultimately responsible for the outbursts of student unrest two decades ago and
for the continuing sense of alienation which still afflicts higher education. An
education which to a large extent took students out of 'community education'
and placed them in the isolation of élitist institutions fired an explosive reaction
against that very community. Although the protest is now much more muted,
students still grope after a new kind of experience in higher education. They see
universities as the agents of 'establishments', including under that umbrella
term the State, the Church, capitalist interests and cultural agencies which
operate in support of these. All the present establishments are bad: they can
only drive the world further into injustice and violence in the last decade of this
century. A protest pinned up in the Sorbonne in 1968 announced: 'The
consumer society must perish by a violent death. The society of alienation must
disappear from history. We are inventing a new and original world. Imagination is seizing power!' The vision still tarries but we may link the 1968

statement with a recent one from a student conference: 'The old idea of a university must be relegated to the dustbin'. Largely because of their individualist and competitive associations, technocratic assumptions about man, society and the natural world have, so the student argument runs, warped experience at its roots. The first aim of the new culture must be 'the subversion of the scientific world view with its entrenched commitment to an egocentric and cerebral mode of consciousness'.[2] 'We do not', said Laing (one of the student prophets), 'need theories so much as the experience that is the source of the theory'.[3]

Here lies a confusion of thought which must be sorted out: 'experience' must not be placed in this absolute opposition to 'theory'. We do not need to repudiate the gains of a scientific methodology which trains in critical analysis and the uses of abstraction. It is ironical that a generation of students trained through a predominantly analytical method should turn the tools of critical analysis against the deficiencies of their education. It remains, nevertheless, a true function of education in every generation to turn a critical scrutiny on the values implicit in the very society which fosters that generation. Our crucial task today is to marry experience and theory, the indwelling perception of whole-ness and the concepts built on a critical study of the parts. From the combination of experience and theory new 'meanings' have to be forged by the next generation. Why is this of such importance? Because we are concerned primarily, not with the forging of precision tools for society nor with the training of academic enquirers, but with the nourishment of whole persons.

So we return to our question: What do students need? Basically, what everyone needs: Power to live their lives with power. 'Power' in this context is a multi-layered word. In the social aspect it can be described as power to make a significant impact on your world, however small or large. This in itself has various aspects: power to be active in serving other people through making, doing, solving problems, leading or following; power to share experiences and thoughts, power to give and receive love; power to commit oneself to long-term causes and loyalties with open-eyed and critical awareness. There is, however, another dimension which interacts at every point with the first. Here we recognize power to explore and in discovery to find wonder and delight; power to create something out of experience and knowledge; power to meet ills and cross-accidents without being defeated by them; power 'to fail without losing composure or confidence';[4] power to worship; power to meet death with dignity.

What we have tried to set down here are the needs of a real person. But growing into a fully personal person is obviously not synonymous with taking a college course or getting an academic qualification. The nourishment of persons is a mysterious process: you cannot evolve a chemical formula for it as for a universal fertilizer. You will meet 'real persons' springing up from under the asphalt of inner cities as often as from the carefully prepared soil of suburban homes or the tranquillities of the countryside. Equally, education cannot 'make a person': it has a more limited role. Its open concern is with the knowledge-business, but we make an act of faith, in setting up educational institutions, that the handing on of a heritage of knowledge will add to the stature of human persons rather than diminish it. If we believe this, we must affirm it fully. But then we have to be sure that the transmission of knowledge is indeed creating the experience through which growing persons can receive nourishment.

So let us consider the transmission of knowledge in terms of five components in the nourishment of persons.

1. Knowledge is for achieving competence in doing
There should be an essential link between acquiring information and transforming it into actions which are forms of service. The link is partly through the mastery of tools and skills, but more subtly through the translation of 'theoretical' into 'applied' at every stage. The duty and function of education to provide competent persons was long ago stated in the Oxford Bidding Prayer: 'And that there may never be wanting a succession of persons duly qualified for the service of God in Church and State . . .'. But today we do not have a simple equation between higher education and useful career to deal with. The old expectation that a successful course in H.E. would automatically lead to an honourable professional job is no longer certain. Inability to use the skills you have learned and even inability to get a job at all are prospects students have to face. The economic situation presses cruelly on developing persons who need to find some form of real service in order to find themselves. Frustrated by a society which does not seem to want them, some young people appear to repudiate social obligation and seem not to want to serve anyone. *Au fond* I believe they *do*, because counting for someone significant in the community is necessary for finding their own identity. I recall a young apprentice who was observed pointing out a certain car in the showroom window and announcing to his pals: '*Thats* the car I'm helping to make'. But if society seems to have rejected them, they will reject any claims to their service. There is no clear way out of this present evil in the job situation, unless we have the courage to widen our concept of 'work' beyond the traditional 'earning a living'. By 'work' I mean here any useful activity which is performed primarily for the service of other people as well as oneself. If the time absorbed by, and the significance of earning one's living is more and more reduced, or even denied altogether to some, then there must be created other communal outlets for the real 'work impulse'. The facile and implicitly selfish alternative of education for leisure is no answer at all.

Competence, then, is a legitimate goal in education, but there is a caveat to be entered here. Competence implies the ability to find successful answers to problems. Problem-solving is the criterion of success. In a striking lecture Bishop John Taylor castigates 'our devouring worship of success'. He questions the prevalent view that human life 'consists of a narrowing down of the entire experience of the world to an answering of questions and a solving of problems. It is the illusion of technique. All our desired successes consist in the answers we know and the solutions we can work out. . . . If a person or a government or an institution does not solve the problem then there has been a failure'.[5] In the face of the prevailing view that every problem has a solution if we can only find it, Taylor asks: 'Do we dare to grasp the truth that the human creature needs problems more than he needs solutions? We are beings that thrive on questions but grow sickly on answers . . .'[6] Within the whole rich range of human responses to life competence to cope successfully has a limited value.

Nevertheless, education has a real responsibility in this area, first to make clear the connection between learning and responsible activity, and secondly, to place the acquisition of competence in a wider setting than that of just securing a good job. Here the employment market also has an educational role. A report states that 'industry has almost totally failed to tap the streak of idealism in young people by showing the importance of industry in the wealth-creating process' (*The Times*, 30/11/85). This is a remark both perceptive and revealing: perceptive in spotting the latent idealism of the young, but revealing in its naive belief that this can be channelled into 'wealth-creating' *tout simple*. 'Wealth for what or for whom?' many would ask. A vision of world-service, especially to the disadvantaged, comes nearer to the ideal to which they would respond. Flexibility and vision are needed to see how information, technologies, skills, can be used for service in new ways. To quote Bishop Taylor again:[7]

> Versatility will be worth far more to them than specialization. A good groundwork of technical skills – electrical, mechanical and constructional, with simple book-keeping and business management, should be the birthright of every pupil, however dull or bright, since all should be able to make a job for themselves rather than waiting to be given one. . . . Rather than posing questions to which there is only one correct answer, or setting problems for which a classic solution has long ago been formulated, we should try to devise situations that call for imagination and resourcefulness and which may be dealt with in a great variety of ways. We need the mental equivalent of a good assault course in which, for example, the participants arrive at a deep-flowing river and find awaiting them on the bank a collection of poles, ropes and pulleys. One may knock a raft together, another swings across from a scaffold, and a third decides it is worth the discomfort of a swim. All are different versions of success, and, as in Wonderland, there should be prizes for all.

2. *Knowledge is for human understanding*

We all need to discover who we are, to whom we belong and how we may relate ourselves to other people and to our environment. We have to learn how to open ourselves to new experiences of people and how to enter through imagination into that which is strange, even upsetting, in other people's ideas and experience. A lot of this must be learnt directly through living, but knowledge through books can add a further dimension. For the written word is the storehouse of human memory and we need its riches to interpret our own lives with power. In other words, we need to be nourished on history, in which I include all recorded or remembered human activity, thought and experience right up to the present. We must live our lives forwards but we only understand them backwards and so we need to enter into the past as a living experience. In this aspect education has been called 'a great conversation'.[8]

This is an obvious point where Wants and Needs can appear to clash. The cry for immediate relevance is frequently heard: 'No experience prior to the Second

World War is any use to me', said a student to me in the 1960s. Now the cut-off point will have moved on. This is a very 'instant' and superficial view. In fact, for any one of us, there emerges mysteriously a deeper relevance, when out of any past age some person or group speaks to our imagination and we take their piece of experience into our own. Our phrase 'latching on' means establishing a relationship with, or mingling something of yourself with this new material for experience. There is an alchemy here that can transmute dead lumps of knowledge into pure gold. Sometimes we are amazed at the way the magic works. It can begin with distaste or repulsion. I remember a Californian student who came to class without the 'report' on Dante's *Monarchia* which had been assigned to her. 'I can't do it', she said, 'I hate his ideas so much'. But her imagination got caught and she ended by urging us on to hold extra sessions in order to finish the *Commedia*: 'I've got to get to Paradise', she said. Again, a study of medieval heretics and dissidents proved to be good 'growing material': behind the objective study from documents of the attitudes of both heretics and authorities, one could sense the twentieth-century minds reflecting on their own dissidences and their resolution.

The Bible is a deep well of human living. Anyone brought up to know its greatest books draws up from memory bucket-fulls of experience that speak to our condition. Consider, from the Old Testament alone, the archetypal explorer, Abraham, going out he knew not whither to seek a city; Jacob, wrestling with the great Unknown in the dark; Joseph, the compassionate one in an envious family; David, sparing his enemy and pouring out the precious water of human love before God; Elijah, stirred out of self-pity to meet a vision; Job, questioning God; the passionate Jonah proved wrong. More especially do writings which record men's encounters with God ring a bell in this age of seekers after an ultimate truth. Thus we recall Isaiah's reaction to the glory of God's presence: 'I am a man of unclean lips . . .' yet 'Here am I, send me' (Isaiah 6:5, 8); or Jeremiah's desperate attempt to escape the role he must play: 'Ah, Lord God! behold I cannot speak, for I am a child' (Jeremiah 1; 6); or the awesome command to Ezekiel: 'Son of man, stand upon thy feet, and I will speak unto thee'.

A passage from C. S. Lewis on reading English Literature when he was still an unbeliever points up a 'relevance' he was unwilling to acknowledge:[9]

> The most religious (writers) . . . were clearly those on whom I could really feed. On the other hand, those writers who did not suffer from religion and with whom in theory my sympathy ought to have been complete . . . all seemed a little thin . . . 'tinny' . . . There seemed to be no depth in them. They were too simple. The roughness and density of life did not appear in their books.

The point here is not so much a good mark for the Christians as the unexpected relevance of works Lewis thought would be unpalatable. A significant trend since the Second World War has been a turning-back to historical themes by playwrights who wish to encapsulate some aspect of the human predicament and find the 'speech' of history more powerful than that of contemporary situations. To give only two examples, Robert Bolt chose Sir Thomas More, *A Man for all Seasons*, because he wanted to high-light the theme of a consistent integrity in this age when the enduring *I* sometimes seems to be disintegrating. In his preface he reflects on our inability to understand More's position because there is so little sense of anything abiding within ourselves: 'We feel – we know – the self to be an equivocal commodity'. Yet here was a man who, though he 'gratefully accepted the shelter of his society' was prepared to be 'thrust out into the terrifying cosmos' because the meaning of his own person was so deep within him that he could not forswear it. 'It may be', says Bolt wistfully, 'that a clear sense of the self can only crystallize round something transcendental.'[10] Here, indeed, was history speaking to our present condition. In quite another vein Peter Shaffer's play *Amadeus* searches out the whole mystery of the gift of genius poured out so unstintingly on Mozart. The choice of plays for performance in the 'serious' theatre and the involvement of actors and audiences again underlines the relevance of past experience even from the remote past. Thus the National Theatre was packed, night after night, for the long triology of the *Oresteia*, with its unfolding of the archaic yet burningly topical theme of blood-feud and violent revenge versus reconciliation. *Peer Gynt* is a strange play to perform, yet it recently inspired a deeply convincing performance from students who pursued the fleeting, but urgent, question: 'Who am I?' with great fervour right through the kaleidoscopic scenes of Peer's experiences. Reflecting on this strange relationship we have with the past, C. S. Lewis made a percipient point:[11]

> I do not think you need fear that the study of a dead period . . . need prove an indulgence in nostalgia or an enslavement to the past. In the individual life as the psychologists have taught us, it is not the remembered but the forgotten past that enslaves us. I think the same is true of society. To study the past does indeed liberate us from the present, from the idols of our own market place. But I think it liberates us from the past too. I think no class of men are less enslaved to the past than historians. The unhistorical are usually, without knowing it, enslaved to a fairly recent past.

The treasure-house of human experience is vast. It would be a deprivation of the first order to have to live two-dimensionally, without a richly stored memory. Whatever we take from the past with imagination and sympathy, whatever in it moves us to compassion, exultation, terror or awe, whatever we make our own out of it – all this adds a dimension to our lives and sometimes even gives us the very language in which to articulate our own experience. Moreover, the past shows us human persons facing suffering, disaster, and death, and these are necessities of the human condition with which we have to come to terms, for we seek to evade them at our peril.

So knowledge is for enlarging experience and the understanding of who man is. As a Harvard study of business men's needs rather surprisingly put it: 'People need well developed hearts. Knowledge is for the nourishment of hearts.'

3. Knowledge is for sustaining the experience of 'difference' in the search for truth

The myth of the Tower of Babel teaches us that language can be either a vehicle of communication or a source of great confusion. It is a moot point as to which is winning today. The global village in which we all live brings everyone capable of listening, looking or reading up against a Babel of voices speaking the languages of different races, religions, political creeds and class-consciousnesses. Many educationalists – certainly in schools – are dedicated to inculcating tolerance, understanding, sympathy between the members of their multi-racial class-rooms and on a global scale to giving, through world history, geography and religious knowledge, an imaginative experience of 'difference' which will foster a sense of world citizenship. Much of this work is highly successful at the school stage and some, perhaps many, carry a sensitive world perspective into later life. But over against these successes we must set the disturbing phenomenon of young people (and adults) arrayed in embattled groups against one another. The 'difference' may be only the triviality of football rivalries but throughout the world there are the much more deeply divisive issues of tribe, sect, political ideology and so forth. This evil which is poisoning societies seems to be exacerbated by the conversion of language into a weapon of emotional defence. Language becomes basically a mechanism for establishing and defending security. So an ideological fortress is constructed – and I use 'ideology' here in the extreme sense of a system of ideas which admits no possibility of an alternative vision of truth – in which individuals or members of groups enclose themselves. They cut themselves off from communication in the sense of entertaining any different points of view or ideas: they can only shout slogans at those outside from the ramparts of their fortress.

Why does this ideological imprisonment afflict so many of the younger generation? Understanding the disease is essential: ham-handed attempts to suppress the students who try to block unacceptable lecturers (or fellow students), or to cut grants to Student Unions in the name of academic freedom get nowhere. The insecurity which causes closed minds is real and if our educational aim is to show that the ideological remedy is spurious we must attack it with full sympathy for the human condition out of which it arises.

For our remedy, admittedly, means taking the hard and the high road. Our academic creed is that knowledge is for discovering truth, not for battening down the hatches in the storm. But this is a painful, often costing experience. At odds with the exploring instinct there is a great urge in the human spirit to remain cosily within a 'home' furnished with well-known, sometimes well-loved, concepts which together form a reassuring view of life. It is hard to expose treasured ideas to question, to entertain disturbing new ones, to hold the tension between one's personal position and that of the individual or group with whom one is seeking communication. Yet the essence of the search for truth lies precisely in this 'open-ness', in this intention to listen carefully and to understand as fully as possible before making counter-reply. Higher education offers, *par excellence*, the time and place for learning to live with conflicting ideas and for building up the integrity to seek the truth at any cost. As teachers, it is our responsibility to engage students in real discourse, with each other, with books and with ourselves. Here, in the academic context, a basic tenet of our creed is that all issues of values or faith are 'open', no holds barred, no *ex cathedra* pronouncements permissible. On matters of 'fact' we may be entitled to speak 'with authority' – remembering the large grey areas where fact shades into value – but if we are drawn into statements of our own belief this can only be as witnesses to personal experience.

The Spanish philosopher Unamuno, as interpreted by John Wyatt, has striking things to say about the role of conflict in the process of real learning. 'This philosophy', says Wyatt, 'rests on interaction with others.'[12] His message is worth listening to because it is about intellectual energy, about the energy to continue, rather than the 'gloom that disables', even about painful learning which is joy. 'Instead of an epistemology of sameness, unity and identification, we have offered here a proposal for pursuing contradictions, oppositions, tensions and, in short, living with risk and agony.' Reflecting on this philosophy, Wyatt observed that 'the certainties, the forthrightness and clear-eyed knowledge of where you are going, so beloved of management people with nerves of steel and objectives of polished brass may be the very characteristics which oppose some of the work that a university or college is best equipped to do. . . . A tragic vision may in the end be an enriching vision whereas other more apparently optimistic success stories may turn out to be illusions, corrupting the diverse drama of learning.'

This way is harder but the prize infinitely more satisfying than the prize of safety. What I have called the 'experience of difference' breaks up moulds of thought that had set too hard, enlarges human understanding, gives sparkle and the excitement of the unexpected to exploration and enables us to entertain, if not adopt, many 'friends' of infinite variety. Above all, it is through 'open-ness' to conflict that we can attain a degree of integrity. Dr Anthony Kenny's *A Path from Rome* eloquently conveys the agonies of philosophical doubt engendered by an academic environment, but also the satisfaction of integrity finally won.[13] But I come back to the problem of the psychological demand which the pursuit of academic openness makes. In the last decades of the twentieth century is the pursuit of this confessedly 'liberal' way too much to ask for? Is it therefore almost wholly unsuccessful? The question is open, but if there is any academic faith it is centred on this belief in openness as a fundamental in scholarship as in education. I take for granted all the relativities which have modified the original liberal ideal of the open mind, but these have not reduced the concept to nothingness.

4. *Knowledge is for enjoyment*
As we have already argued, this is the key to the whole process. We could almost say that the 'end' of all knowledge is enjoyment. The disciplines of learning skills, the drudgery, the stresses and strains along the road certainly have their importance in the making of a person and, of course one may undertake some unpalatable study as a matter of duty or necessity, but learning devoid of *any* element of enjoyment, present or in view, is simple dreariness. For enjoyment in the sense in which I am using it is the source of vitality.

Let us analyse its nature more closely. It has an element of exhilaration in achievement: *I* have made this; *I* have cracked this problem; *I* have created this pattern of knowledge; *I* have communicated it in clear and elegant language. But the root of enjoyment goes much deeper. We respond – and enjoy our achievement in responding – to what is already there. The root of all delight lies in the given-ness of things. We will consider the theological implications of that statement later, but however we seek to explain it, this is a universal experience. Our curiosity is stimulated by the strange and puzzling, our sense of beauty by the order, symmetry and artistry of what we encounter, our emotions by the grandeur and the tragedy of the human story or the magnificence of the physical universe. Traherne remembered his ecstasy as a child:[14]

> All appeared new and strange at the first, inexpressibly rare and delightful and beautiful. I was a little stranger which at my entrance into the world was saluted and surrounded with innumerable joys. . . . The corn was orient and immortal corn. . . . The green trees . . . transported and ravished me.

I recently watched just such a transport of delight as a child of under two discovered fir-cones for the first time.

But exploring with abandon is dangerous. A small child will do it:[15]

> He is not afraid of being belittled by his discoveries because he accepts his own littleness as one of the principal facts of his existence. He is not afraid that there will be more unexplained territory beyond what he is so laboriously exploring now. He is not afraid of discovering more than he can manage: for him the world is not a very manageable place anyhow.

But later all kinds of cautions put the brake on. We want a manageable world. We want a short cut to solutions. We want instant success. All these curb our desire to be explorers and dim our sense of wonder.[16]

> Reality must be seen as shallow so as to be easily comprehended: it must be rendered unimpressive lest it overawe. Let things have neither height nor depth nor breadth, or we shall become proportionally insignificant.

Yet Traherne speaks of the 'felicity' which should be the 'end of all university education'. To students who – full of anxieties about passing examinations and getting jobs – shrink from exploration there is a gospel to be preached: sail out into the open seas and find your felicity in the riches on unexpected shores. And it is for us, the teachers, to propel them out of harbour if they linger too long. Perhaps we should be more explicit about the rewards of exploration. Our only 'engine force' here is our own excitement and enjoyment, remembering Traherne's sad comment: 'But there was never a teacher who did expressly teach felicity.'[17] We have an over-riding responsibility to transmit our belief in the worthwhileness of the exploration to a new generation.

The essence of this enjoyment lies in the fact that we do not make it all ourselves. No human-being is absolute creator: all of us are in some sense artists or craftsmen working with given materials. To take as of right tarnishes and dims all we work on; to take as a gift unseals the springs of vitality. Seeing life solely in terms of rights to be claimed can make it utterly sterile, producing an unsatisfied, frustrated individual. Seeing life in terms of gifts can be a fructifying experience, generating the desire and the power to live by giving gifts. So the vitality engendered by this gift of felicity can spread into the springs of all our actions. The pursuit of competence itself can become a felicitous as well as a useful activity. So we can pour into human understanding and relationships a more generous giving of ourselves. Enjoyment liberates into new activity.

The intellectual and artistic forms of enjoyment which fall within the province of Higher Education do not, of course, exhaust its possibilities, nor does Higher Education have a monopoly even of these. But we who teach are the custodians of particular life-giving experiences; though some will find them without, or in spite of us, they are in our gift as teachers of students. Not all, alas, will be in a fit state to respond: their *malaise* may go too deep. But Higher Education can and should be a liberating experience.

5. *Knowledge is for Contemplation*
Enjoyment shades into contemplation and wonder and these are inescapable elements in the act of knowing. Even Francis Bacon admitted that wonder was the seed of knowledge and Einstein wrote: 'whoever remains unmoved, whoever cannot contemplate or know the deep shudder of the soul in enchantment, might as well be dead, for he has already closed his eyes upon life'.[18] 'Learning without wonder is no learning', says Melvyn Matthews, 'since desire and yearning are not aroused. If desire and yearning are not part of the process of education, then no education takes place; nothing is revealed and nothing remembered.'[19] Contemplation is sustained attention and attention to what is outside ourselves is the mainspring of living. Therefore what we attend to and how we attend are of crucial importance. As Iris Murdoch says in *The Sovereignty of Good*, 'Our capacity for action depends on the quality of our habitual objects of attention.'[20] Here once again we see how falacious a sharp dichotomy between contemplation and action can be. Attention to trivial things, like cleaning our teeth, fills much of our ordinary days, but the 'grand' actions of any person – acts of love or sacrifice, imaginative leaps of the mind or acts of creation – must draw their vitality from the range of grand or spacious objects of contemplation which have enriched the spirit. So the thrust of the educational process must be away from the confined range of attention to trivialities towards a focus on those things which can become a powerful source of energy. This energy, as we have already seen, comes from outside ourselves: the activity of contemplation is the opposite of an inward-looking focus on the aims and images of the self; the latter imprisons the spirit within a fantasy system; the former liberates through attending to an outside reality. This statement, of course, leaves open the question of what is meant by 'reality' and, in this context, that open-ness is intentional. We may tie ourselves into philosophical knots trying to define reality but experientially we know from whence we draw our inspiration. Its sovereignty is indisputable as it commands our response. Here a funny little remark of a seven-year old boy points up the difference between trivial and

important objects of attention: admonished by grandmother to 'pay attention to your feet' in the bath, he replied: 'I can't pay attention to my feet; they can't speak'. 'Attention' implied important communication to him.

It is important communication that educationalists must constantly seek to approach through all the stages of teaching. Trivia abound on the road but, whether in planning courses, delivering lectures, conducting classes, seminars, tutorials, our attention has to be on the ultimate meanings which are flowing into students' minds. First, the authentic voices must be allowed to speak: this is 'knowledge for its own sake'. But the process of contemplation does not end there. In the second stage all the excitement, stimulus and wonder of listening or seeing can be transmuted by reflection into a developing sense of what it means to be human. The transition from the first to the second stage was long ago expressed in the briefest terms by the Psalmist: 'When I consider thy heavens . . . what is Man that Thou are mindful of him . . . ?' (8:3, 4) Reflection here is the road to wisdom, the wisdom that Nicholas Maxwell seeks in his book *From Knowledge to Wisdom*.[21] But, once again, he makes too sharp a distinction between the pursuit of knowledge for its own sake, which he sees as bad, and the pursuit of wisdom which is good. The philosophy which he is attacking is the sterile, so-called 'objective' accumulation of factual knowledge, the pursuit of which has set a false so-called scientific objective and taken higher education down the wrong road. But the energy-giving exhilaration of 'finding truth for its own sake' is precisely the inspiration which fuels reflection and sets us on the road to wisdom.

Our role is the enabling one of guiding students towards the discovery of this road. But it is too subtle to be pinned down in practical suggestions or reforms. It means, in the first place, that we ourselves have to be contemplating creatures, reflecting not only on the meaning of life in general, but on the particularly way our own knowledge may be viewed in the context of the human condition. We may personally till a very small allotment in the field of knowledge but we must do so remembering always that it is a 'fair field full of folk'.[22] Secondly, we must be alert to all the resonances of our own subject matter. We can, in a sense, either relay or stifle the voices that speak to the seeker in the way we handle themes. Thirdly, we should make time and opportunity for the exploration of connections between the material under study and both other parts of the field of knowledge and the conditions of present living. We must even be prepared, where possible, to entertain such red herrings as 'What is all this in aid of?' and 'Why are we here?'. Fourthly, we have to enable the processes of fuller reflection by providing various kinds of opportunity, informal or organized, for more sustained meditation or contemplation of 'meanings'.

There are many levels of reflection all the way up to the contemplation of the most high. What this final level can embrace is a deeply personal question. Iris Murdoch sees it as the contemplation of 'perfection', goodness or beauty and speaks in terms of great art. Its essence lies in its transcendence: 'What is truly beautiful is "inaccessible" and cannot be possessed or destroyed . . . the sovereign idea cannot be taped – it is in its very nature that we cannot get it taped. It always lies beyond and it is from this beyond that it exercises its authority.' But, she affirms, 'great psychological power derives from the mere idea of the transcendent object. . . . The idea of perfection moves and possibly changes us because it inspires love in the part of us that is most worthy'.[23] So the true artist is obedient to a conception of perfection which is always beyond him but to which his work is constantly related and re-related. In the sense in which it is used here, the potentiality to be a 'true artist' exists in all of us. This relation is our ultimate purpose in education. But it involves sacrificing what is a cherished delusion among many academics: the possibility of ultimately 'getting everything taped'. The best – because the humblest – scholars know that there is always a limit to the power of knowing. Koestler expresses the sense of the vast, illimitable vision in his phrase 'oceanic wonder'.[24] Wonder and awe are the Alpha and Omega of the activity of knowing.

5

Academic Attitudes

I apologise to my wife for the love affair I have had with my
subject

(from a preface to an academic work)

In writing this book I have often wanted to use the phrase 'academic community', or some such, and have then hesitated and written 'Scholars and students'
instead because there may be no community at all. Do we see our institutions as
single communities of learners sharing at least some common presuppositions,
or as emporia where each snatches what he can off the shelves of knowledge, or –
at best – as bifurcated into two communities of staff and students? There are in
fact two kinds of fragmentation which are destroying the sense of academic
community. The first is the individualism of scholars and of differentiated
faculties, existing in a competitive separatism with few or no bonds between
specialism or opportunities to explore common aims and values. Has the word
'academic' lost its real meaning, signifying scholars who share a purpose, to
become merely a pejorative adjective? If so, individuals, departments, institutions are all the more vulnerable to outside pressures because they share no
common identity. Institutions of higher education can become simply collec-
tions of specialist departments and individuals, open to innumerable temp-
tations because they do not really know what they would go to the stake for.
Secondly, the market model of purveyors and consumers puts, as it were, the
selling counter between teachers and students, creating a transaction increasingly governed by commercial principles. Customers demand; learners
ask. Customers pay cash; learners communicate. The market transaction finds
no place for shared problems, discoveries, enthusiasms.

And yet the older model of the guild which shaped European universities at
their inception is still present and valid. It is highly significant that just at this
moment when various pressures are undermining it the Rectors of European
Universities are embarking on a tremendous enterprise to explore and revive
the true traditions of these institutions. They constitute a unique growth in the
history of cultures. They were not modelled on classical precedents nor did they
follow the guru/disciple tradition of the East. The basic concept of the guild was
the passage by stages from apprenticeship to mastership and theoretically every
apprentice was a potential master. Of course in practice many did not attain the
full 'fellowship'. In the guild which became the *universitas* the apprentice stage
might mean the education of mere schoolboys but nonetheless they were part of

a community of learners, expecting to reach the journeyman/bachelor stage when they would be admitted to a limited teaching role, and in many cases attaining the mastership which signified entry into full membership. Whether or not they remained for the academic life of the doctor or went into one of the careers for which the universities provided literate personnel, they had been admitted to the membership of a common enterprise. Although the processes of teaching and learning are now so different, this is still our true model.

The first strength of the guild model lies in its concept of a community of masters. This stands four-square, on the one hand, against prostitution of aims by undue outside pressures, and, on the other, against excesses of irresponsible individualism inside. It can only uphold this solidarity if sufficient members share a common understanding of their value-imperatives in research and a common sense of their responsibilities in teaching. It has recently been claimed that today disciplines have become so specialist and professions so technical that they can hardly be said to share any common values. This has to be challenged. They may be kept too far below the surface, but all scholarly activities, by their very nature, share certain intrinsic values, such as openness in the quest, persistence in following the clues and integrity in recording and communicating their findings. Corporately, the 'fellowship' has to stand for these explicitly; individually, members have to accept commitment to these as a limitation on freedom. Several writers of today see two opposed forces pulling the university apart. They can be defined in these terms: 'One is the social representation of the existence of the free and sovereign will of the self; the other represents the inverse affirmation that, since no common principles of interpersonal behaviour can be rationally grounded, the will of an organisation (i.e. from outside) must be imposed to limit and channel the arbitrariness of individual choice'.[1] So the alternatives appear to be that either universities must sell themselves to outside corporations, or try fruitlessly to remain 'playgrounds for liberals who would eventually find themselves . . . deprived of their ability to play'.[2] Facing this impending judgement, Melvyn Matthews calls for the resolution of the dilemma in 'a richer, deeper community of virtue . . . , a refusal to divorce the pursuit of goodness from the pursuit of academic excellence.' The 'practice' of the academic guild must embrace the internal 'goods' that motivate its members, that bind them together and that form part of the tradition they must pass on. 'Who and what academics are and can be cannot be separated from the academic pursuit. . . . Who and what my teacher is and wishes to become impinges directly upon what he chooses to teach. Universities cannot afford to divorce who and what their members are from the academic task'.[3]

This brings us straight to the second strength of the guild concept: its emphasis on the apprentice as a learner *in the same craft*. The argument against this approach of trying to take students into the enterprise of scholarship is that for the majority today higher education is only a passing phase in their lives. Permanent involvement is only for the few, so what is the point of trying to give them the freedom of academia? We shall in the last chapter be discussing Alasdair MacIntyre's concept of engagement in a 'practice' under a 'master' as crucial education in the 'virtues' appropriate to that practice. Students leaving higher education should (in a healthy society) be entering into many different 'practices', each of which ought, through its own coherence and virtues, to impart its own brand of excellence. That, of course, is an ideal picture, but – whether or not it exists – we are not prevented from seeking to prepare them for such experiences by admission to our own full practice. Its 'mystery' – to use the medieval word for the qualities of a specific craft – lies in the energy, toughness and integrity with which activities of the mind are pursued, in the persistence with which fresh starts are made when false trails have to be abandoned, in the generosity with which insights and information are shared and in the cooperation which enriches enterprises of learning. These experiences and qualities cry out to be carried into a world of activities beyond academia along with the useful skills which students have acquired there.

But the view that an academic institution can, in any sense, become a community of learners faces a fundamental challenge which rest on the assumption that 'scholar's knowledge' is something quite different in kind from 'students' knowledge'. Desmond Ryan, coming up against the phenomenon that academic teachers are not interested in courses on student learning, finds the reason in their exclusive focus on a discipline:[4]

> When we ask higher education lecturers, even the greater part of secondary school teachers, what they do, the answers are almost inevitably of the kind 'I teach metallurgy/French/psychology'. The discipline or subject is what commands their loyalty . . . success in the discipline is what confirms their identity . . . success means success in research – in some science faculties, to confess an interest in educational concerns is to indicate that one no longer has what it takes to keep up with the research frontier.

Dr Ryan claims that they are 'dominated, even deformed, by their discipline and its ethos', for they do not operate with any concept of the unity of knowledge. 'Each subject culture, far from being one branch on a great tree of knowledge, is more like a separate species of plant, struggling each against all for light, space and nutrients.' Thus 'disciplines are highly structured social institutions . . . the edges of disciplines are well policed; work in the margins has difficulty in getting a hearing and the inter-disciplinary individual or institution lives under the fear of all genetic "sports", mass attack by "normal" scientists or scholars. When a lecturer looks at a class, this highly differentiated world view is what he or she looks through'. On this interpretation lecturers' knowledge equals research knowledge. This type of knowledge is 'their working material – securing it, clarifying it, integrating it, sharing it, destroying it. Skill with knowledge got them the job, not skill with students.' The students themselves are seen as 'onlookers at a public re-enactment of hours, days of private struggle in study, library or laboratory', while 'As a teacher, the typical academic's "crime" is that he treats students as though they were academics too . . . as though for them too the tastiest treat was knowledge in the raw, chunks of it to cut their teeth on'. This is educationally unsound for those who 'will never again, if they can help it, meet knowledge in the raw'.

All this assumes that the typical academic lives and moves and has his being on a way-out frontier where he digs up and handles nothing but 'raw knowledge'. But is there any such sharp distinction between 'raw' and some other sort of knowledge – presumably pre-digested – which students want and need? Whatever may be true for the sciences, the picture for the humanities – and possibly for the social sciences – is quite different. There is always a frontier, of course, but it is not fixed; it is more like that mysterious frontier in some fairy tales which ebbs and flows; sometimes the tide runs far out and sometimes it washes right up to the shore and to the paddling pools. In other words, the subject matter in the humanities is such that the research frontier may happen to lie right across the familiar ground of a well-worn teaching topic which is due for re-assessment, or an academic may simply be in the business of re-interpreting an old theme. Research and teaching material get inextricably mixed. Indeed, it can be the case that a question raised by a student can suddenly open up a whole new problem or possibility for research in an area where all had been thought settled. It is impossible to draw a clear distinction between knowledge in the raw and pre-digested tablets fed to students, nor do I know what the evidence is that students can only learn when fed the latter. In the humanities at any rate research and teaching material are inter-related in many subtle ways.

But the indictment goes further in suggesting that academics, by the very nature of their own training, can only be concerned in the process of making other scholars. The process of becoming an academic is seen as one of socialization: 'Academics come to their role as if to an inheritance. This they are prepared for by living in the relevant cultural world. . . . Teaching means initiating newcomers into that world, sharing its meanings. They know what it is they want to share; when they teach someone who really wants to share it, the greatest gift they can pass on is their methods for attacking ignorance and constructing meanings.'[5] Thus, so the argument goes, 'training' to teach students is irrelevant. How far is it true that academics are actually inhibited from comprehending the learning processes of students as preparation for roles in the outside world? There will, or course, always be some misplaced researchers who get thrust into teaching but cannot escape from the bounds of their esoteric preoccupations. But in general, have academics been so conditioned (one might almost say neutered) as to be devoid of a basic interest in human nature? Yet the foundation of any teaching skill consists precisely in this: an interest in and sensitivity to the minds of other human beings and a desire to communicate with them. Skill can be improved by techniques and here may lie the value of courses on how students learn. But in higher education – as distinct from lower education – where relationships are more or less between adults, techniques matter less than experience in communicating with other human beings in one's own style and sensitivity to the many subtle and differing ways in which those humans absorb and make their own what has been offered. The phenomenon of the idiosyncratic teacher who breaks all the rules but is unforgettable points to a truth which transcends technique. One recalls Lord Fulton's testimony to his teachers at Balliol: 'We never doubted that we had first claim upon them'.

One triangular model of the professional task of the academic teacher has been proposed as a continuous three-way switching of attention between disciplinary content, student and the educational sciences which purport to relate the two together. This is surely the wrong triangle. The two agents (teacher and student) who form the base of the learning triangle are oblivious of education techniques when, in relationship, their 'focal awareness' is totally concentrated on the third point of the triangle, the subject. This may or may not be relevant ultimately to the profession which the student will pursue later, but for the moment its own 'worth' dominates the mind's attention. It is not the 'educational sciences' which relate student and 'disciplinary content' together, but the teacher's personal commitment to what he is doing. A teacher's 'indwelling' of his subject can be so persuasive as to draw a student into the effort to experience the same kind of meaning. 'He rightly saw that the job of the lecturer was not to prove theorems, but to prove that theorems were worth proving' was the testimony of a memorial address on a distinguished mathematician.[6] There is a chemistry of human communication going on here which works because it is unregulated and unmonitored. This originates in the intellectual passion which – according to Polanyi – motivates the real scholar/teacher and which he/she is 'under authority' to communicate: 'Our culture has been built up by this passionate thought, and young people who give themselves to it live the emotions it teaches them to feel'.[7]

But the reference to personal commitment takes us once more on to this dangerous ground of suspected subjectivity. What *is* a teacher committed to? His or her subject – yes. But Melvyn Matthews implies that the 'internal goods' of a teacher are more personal and embrace more than academic virtues: 'who and what he/she is must enter into the (teaching) relationship'. Many teachers would repudiate this vigorously, since anything approaching intimations of personal conviction has the taint of propaganda. There is a built-in resistance to any explicit discussion of personal values. Yet, commenting on the inhibitions which keep such convictions buried, Professor Basil Mitchell has cleared the ground in an authoritative statement:[8]

> Commitment and impartiality are not antithetical; hence the individual can be both committed to a philosophy of life (whether religious or not) and yet fair in his assessment of evidence and arguments against it. If this were not so we should face a forced choice between (a) an unreasoning dogmatism incapable of impartiality and (b) perpetual ineffectiveness through a continuous suspension of judgement. Most people in academic life are both committed and impartial, otherwise rational academic progress would be impossible. What is true of the individual is also true of the institution.

A key phrase in this statement is 'perpetual ineffectiveness'. A teacher who continually puts up smoke screens to evade serious issues of judgement, purpose, belief, probably does not bamboozle his students into thinking that he is impartial, but sets up the model of a weak, indecisive or escapist character. Young people need and enjoy the impact of exactly the opposite kind of character: the person whose judgements are formed by reasoned beliefs and who presents the reality that to live is to make choices and to make them open-eyed. A famous Old Testament episode states this age-old challenge in dramatic form. Moses is putting the point to the Israelites in the name of God: 'See, I have set before you this day life and good, and death and evil. . . . therefore choose life.'[9] Presenting the necessity of choice does not imply either giving a definition of 'life' and 'death' or directing the choice a certain way. Indeed, the educational imperative can be expressed simply in the words: 'Therefore choose'.

Returning to Dr Ryan's analysis, the judgement that academics cocoon themselves in their own specialism against any traffic with the outside world really bites. His paper is 'a plea for a greater all-round self-awareness, to enable the academic vocation to survive in educational institutions, where it is now most endangered'. To most outsiders academic attitudes are incomprehensible, obscured by the use of such arcane phrases as 'the pursuit of truth' or 'knowledge for its own sake'. But the central motivation which drives the academic's engine of the mind is, in many respects, the same as the force which drives a practical engineer to get to the bottom of a machine problem, or a good business manager to seek all possible openings for his product. Energy of mind and enterprise in action are the same everywhere. What tends to set the academic apart is that his energy is directed towards abstract or theoretical questions and his activity does not look like work. A charlady once said: 'It's nice to see Dr X really *working*', as she surveyed the back of a scholar bent double in the garden. It is both the long-term character of academic labour and its lack of physical strenuousness which make for lay scepticism and encourage the suspicion that 'real scholars' – as distinct from practical researchers – are luxuries we cannot afford.

As an urgent problem this question of outside disbelief in what academics are doing is a new one. In the past universities were acknowledged as places for an élite, cut off in the pursuit of their mysteries from ordinary life, and it did not much matter what people 'outside' thought. It is obvious that this is no longer the case. When taxpayers pay, they have the right to – call the tune? be initiated into the mystery? or a bit of both? It is now quite clear that institutions of higher education are and ought to be accountable to the community through its various controlling agencies. But the concept of accountability needs careful examination. 'Accountability means meeting other people's standards', said David Jenkins (now Bishop of Durham), in his inaugural lecture as professor of theology at Leeds.[10] In the first chapter we looked at some of the standards and attitudes demanded by society: minds directed towards the creation of wealth, skills exercised in practical implementations, capabilities turned towards social needs. These demands are undeniable and they can certainly create a tension between academicism and instrumentalism. But they do not constitute the whole story. In the first place, as we have argued, there are qualities which are of the very essence of pure academic activity which can make students better performers when they plunge into 'practical situations'. In the second place, it is folly for the leaders of our community to set their sights on narrow, short-term objectives in learning, when long-term academic projects which at present look entirely theoretical promise a rich harvest in the next generation. But here an act of faith is demanded and if we are to ask for it, we must interpret our purposes and hopes more fully to the outsider. The true passion of the academic to follow the leads wherever they go is finally a genuine gift to the community, but it is one for which he is accountable and this accountability lies partly in the duty to interpret the 'goods' which flow from his work.

It lies also in a rigorous discipline against self-indulgence in scholarship. Perhaps the form in which this has been in the past most obvious to the outsider has been the promotion of research on *trivia* and indulgence towards students who want to linger comfortably within the academic community doing any piece of research, instead of making their contribution to society outside. The accumulation of information is not the same thing as the pursuit of knowledge, yet too often they are identified. A vast academic industry in the collection and purveyance of information has been built up. Most academics do not question the importance of this. Yet the remark of a research student – 'What will be the result of my research? Just one more article in a learned journal for the poor wretched student of the future to read' – makes one pause for thought, even while recognising that this is a caricature. Is it not the case that too much undigested or trivial information gets into print? In the obsession with information, does not 'knowledge' sometimes elude us, meaning by 'knowledge' information transmuted by the processes of assessment, reflection and judgement? The true academic purpose becomes terribly vulnerable when outsiders can point to what seem trivial or petti-fogging pieces of research. Yet we get into deep water trying to distinguish between the trivial and the valuable. A recent example of the drive to collect every detail of information, however minute, has been M. St. Clare Byrne's fifty-year labour on her monumental edition of the Lisle Letters. At any point the judgement might have been made that a lot of this detail was of little value, yet the whole has been acclaimed as the portrait of an age which enriches the human understanding of a far wider section of the community than just specialists in the Tudor period. In the long run we have to persuade the community at large to make an act of faith in what the academic is doing, since only the scholar can make the judgement as to the 'worthwhileness' of what he chooses. But we cannot ask for this act of faith unless we are deeply conscious of our dependence on the community's labour. The question of who pays in cash is irrelevant at this point. While he follows his self-chosen path the scholar is fed, clothed and housed *through the labour of others*, however he is financed. There is a two-way obligation: the scholar gives the fruits of his intellectual passion to the community; in return, his physical needs are provided for. He must acknowledge the 'given-ness' of his opportunity to follow his own bent.

From some angles of vision it looks as if the walls of academia are very much intact and that the 'outsider' is intent upon making them fall with a blast of government trumpets and taking over the citadel for his own purposes. I believe this is a wrong appraisal of the situation. The signs are that the walls (in the sense of barriers to understanding) have been crumbling by natural erosion for some time. Scholars and teachers are infinitely more aware of their obligations in society generally than they were before the Second World War. This is a truism and there is no need to spell out all the ways in which an interaction between scholars and society now takes place. What is a newer phenomenon can be detected in the signs that more amateurs are getting hooked on their own form of research or learning and therefore are coming closer to an understanding of the academic passion. We shall be discussing these signs more fully in the next chapter. The amateur who has his own private passion for entomology, coin collecting or the history of clocks shares much more with the researching scholar than is often recognized. And his very passion, to which he will devote time, effort and money, demonstrates that 'man does not live by bread alone'. These things, of course, can only be pursued in a relatively well-heeled society. To that extent our hard-nosed advocates of an education directed at wealth-creating are right. But they are wrong in thinking that the needs of human beings today and tomorrow will be wholly met by this narrow concentration. The pressure for 'éducation permanente' and for enabling services to support amateur researchers is going to exercise its own force in breaking down the barriers through greater mutual understanding. The need for 'personal knowledge', as we have attempted to describe it, could bring many people into league with the academic community in a political defence of its true values against the philistines.

If there is any truth in this suggestion, it means that the walls will indeed crumble and the distinction between 'outside' and 'inside' become blurred. But this implies a crucial modification of the academic professional attitude. We still retain something of the medieval guildsman's determination to protect the 'mystery' against interlopers. 'Debasing angels' talk' is a contemptuous way of dismissing the attempt to interpret scholarship to a wider learning public, slamming the doors of the 'mystery' on any enquirers. Today we are called to precisely the opposite attitude, one of open, generous interpretation for all who come asking, an interpretation which mediates without any intrinsic lowering of academic standards. Some of the best scholars have always done this. I remember a conversation with Dame Veronica Wedgewood in which she said she saw her role as what she hoped was 'a top-level popularizer'. The pursuit of ideas and the desire to satisfy curiosity are, we have argued, not the preserve of scholars but common human drives. This point will be expanded in the next chapter. The important thing here is to underline the need for academics – and for intellectuals generally – to reinterpret their role in terms of those who 'enable' allcomers to pursue their drive for personal knowledge.

Finally, the walls are crumbling because imaginative teachers are discovering in many and varied ways that 'experience' forms an integral part of the learning process. This includes both calling on past experience to illuminate present learning processes and experiments in which students go out into social situations to apply and test their theoretical knowledge through practical service. What the growing Study Service movement reveals is the 'large reserve of latent idealism' in young people which cries out to be activated.[11] There is a dynamism of voluntary purpose which is too often divorced from the scholastic learning process. 'What we are trying to do, in promoting study service, is to heal the division between voluntary effort and the curriculum.'[12]

This concept of 'experiential learning', however, comes up against the academic belief that, to undergo the full discipline of studying a subject, the syllabus must be carefully structured in a logical order and the student must rigorously follow this interior logic of the subject itself, rather than the dictates of a personal approach. Experiential learning can be untidy and fragmentary: the bits may never fall into place properly. This is a genuine academic concern, not a defence of an out-dated position. For a fruitful interaction of what we may call academic and community ways of learning, we have to bring the two approaches together in common understanding. Academic teachers must see that a personal approach through experience past or present, generates enthusiasm, involvement, purpose. But those who believe in project methods as the most satisfying mode of education must recognise that the distinction between the amateur and the professional derives largely from the structured approach and disciplined training to which the professional submits, as these are imposed by the subject. The academic attitude here must hold its own ground. Yet a teacher cannot but be open in imaginative sympathy towards the force of experience. In the case of students on a full course it is, of course, the right mixture of the two approaches that has to be worked out. Learning and doing in reality go together, the abstract and the concrete, the individual student and the social group. To send students out at the culminating stage of a course with a disciplined body of knowledge in one area should give a training of the mind which is a permanent asset, but let us not forget the fragmented world of concrete situations into which they go and in which they will have to build up a structure of knowledge from random experiences.

It is a shift but not an abandonment of academic attitudes that we need today. The Tree of Knowledge has for too long been guarded by academics in an enclosed garden. There should be no question of cutting it down or mutilating it by lopping off limbs. The need is to transplant it and root it in the community, in common experience. It will survive and flourish in the future only as it is guarded by all. Knowledge belongs, not to academics, but to all: it lives as it is shared, between teachers and learners and between professional scholars and lay scholars.

6

The Community of Learning and the Community at Large

No man is an island, entire of itself;
Every man is a part of the Continent, a part of the main.

John Donne

The lesson which academics are learning the hard way is that the days of a learned élite supported passively by the labour of the rest are gone for ever. (In China 'mandarin' now means the language of most of the people.) One of the great changes in our age has been the realization by the community at large that it is putting an increasing investment of resources into promoting higher education and supporting the academic life. It follows that returns are now demanded. But what returns? The striking thing is that demands have raised their heads from two very different quarters. For some decades there has been pressure – stronger and more successful in America than in Britain – that the doors of higher education should be opened to a much wider range of people, the older as well as the young. The treasure houses of learning should be open to all whose drive to learn reveals an as yet unrealized potentiality – and again one can take the symbol from China where the people now swarm through the Forbidden City. This pressure leads finally to the demand that all who will, irrespective of ability or qualification, should have a chance. But now, in the days of economic stringency, comes the second pressure from the Capability school asking what returns we should demand from our investment in higher education, and giving the answer themselves: people trained in the capacities needed to produce material wealth. In a crude contrast one could say that the experiment of the Open University has been a shining answer to the first pressure and the expansion of the Polytechnics symbolizes the second pressure – though that statement oversimplifies the purposes of both.

Which 'return' is more vital to the health of the community – a continuing supply of wealth-creating instruments, or of persons who have stretched their capacities and outlook through a full growth in personal knowledge? Or is it a question of both/and in close interaction? The return in terms of practical competence has been clearly delineated in recent pronouncements. We need people skilled in the use of a specialized range of 'tools'; people who, with a general 'tool-training', can adapt quickly to the use of new tools; people trained to seek the most economical and practical answer to a problem rather than its theoretical dissection; people with the bent to apply what they know to society's needs; people with experience in team-work. All this is common-place knowledge. But what place is there for the curiosity which observes and questions the unexpected? Or for the inventive imagination that plucks a new idea out of the air? Where is the contemplative revery that shifts the whole question on to a new plane of understanding? These activities of the spirit cannot be screwed down inside tight little cast-iron models. The community loses even in its immediate economic needs if there is no freedom of the spirit. To tie education too closely to practical aims may kill the goose that lays the golden egg. We must therefore hold the two types of 'return' in a realistic balance.

Precisely because of its much greater elusiveness, the rest of this chapter is focused on the second kind of return, since it is here that a new relationship between academics and the community is crucial. If in any way competent, we know how to teach skills and impart information, but when it comes to what we may well call 'the fruits of the spirit' we often fumble. Yet it is just here that we have a mission to perform. The community still speaks with two voices, for the age-old prejudice that the pursuit of things of the spirit is a preserve for the élite still underlies a common mistrust of 'useless learning'. Against this mind-block the open-ness of learning for all needs to be proclaimed. For it is simply not true that curiosity, imagination, contemplation flower only in certain sorts of social milieu. There have always been those who have burst out of the limits of environment, transcending circumstances in some creative act of the spirit. Today, when the revolution of thought has brought higher education within the range of the community at large, it would be tragic if people were conned into demanding too narrow a range of objectives. The community of learning has to be wide open in all its parts.

Thus our dream for the year two thousand could be that people of all ages over 18 throng the halls of higher education. This could be obtainable, for three social factors, emerging most strongly since the Second World War, point this way. First, the progressive disappearance of unskilled labour and the ever greater demand for a higher and more intellectual competence; secondly, shorter working hours and the creation of more enforced or optional free time; thirdly, the astonishing opening up of fields of knowledge and skills to all who choose to give their attention through the development of the mass media. The first two are obvious; the third calls for some expansion. The number of people one encounters today whose formal education never got beyond age 16 but who are taking excursions into all kinds of fields – history, geography, archaeology, astronomy, physics – is truly remarkable. The 'mysteries' are being opened up. Furthermore, many have been introduced by radio or television to a wider range of language and the use of abstract concepts. People living in many different circumstances play computer games, take part in general knowledge quizzes, visit museums and exhibitions, travel abroad. Once it was the Bible that provided the wider horizon and the cultural liberation of the masses, of a John Bunyan for instance. Now a new general culture is in process of being created out of materials provided by modern technology. All who follow these signals with enthusiasm are potential takers of higher education courses. Of course there will always be a substratum of those who – alas – cannot, or will not expand their powers any further. But a new field is ripening to harvest among potential mature students.

Why are we not reaping as big a harvest here as the American culture does? The first and most obvious reason is that economically we do not provide for 'going back to school' – as they say in the States – nearly as generously. The means for paying your way through college are minimal here and the job situation at present blocks the way. Instead of letting other people into jobs by freeing some for further study, those in employment must hang on grimly. Until recently, a second reason was the rigid structure of our academic courses, mostly of three-year duration, which could not be broken down into units that could be taken at different times, as in the States. The CNAA and the Open University have been largely responsible for changing this situation. 'Modules' or units are now widely used. Something has been lost but much has been gained. Deeper than the economics or mechanics of higher education for mature students, however, lies a subtle distinction between American and English culture. In the States the great effort to weld diverse racial elements into one society has stimulated the drive to bring more and more people into a common heritage of learning, as distinct from the many folk cultures they brought with them. In England (I am not here including Scotland and Wales) a more or less indigenous popular culture existed for long side by side with the intellectual culture of the middle and upper classes. As we have argued already, the class prejudice which kept them apart still operates in far too many people here. In Oklahoma, by contrast, a grain farmer could say quite naturally: 'My grain elevators are full, so I have come back to school for the winter semester.' He was studying philosophy.

I am arguing therefore that the academic community has a mission to the 'layman', using the word here in the sense of one whose focus for living is outside the academic 'clerisy'. Of course he wants much wider opportunities for learning and re-learning skills relevant to the twenty-first century. But beyond these lie those much more subtle needs which, as we have seen, can be expressed in terms of growth through personal knowledge. Defined thus, however, the 'person' seems to stand isolated. Yet we have seen that the true experience of personal knowledge is one of relatedness at various levels. Enrichment of the individual comes through participation in a community of learners or explorers.

At this point educational needs tie in with problems concerning the quality of living in our society. Many would agree with the recent Hibbert lecturer that there is a deep malaise and would seek its cause in the divisiveness engendered by the pursuit of wealth which sets individuals in competitive and 'instrumental' relationships with each other.[1] Change, economic growth, mobility, competing claims to 'rights' are toughening elements which can be defended as pointers to the vitality of a community. But what kind of vitality is this? Its marks are drive, enterprise and greed for more and more material gain to be clutched into private possession. Long ago Dante called this cupidity and denounced it as the root cause of civil strife and violence. Today cupidity is inflamed to an unprecedented degree by every kind of advertising device. It isolates human-beings one from another and tears societies and nations apart in the bitter confrontation of the have-nots with the haves.

We cannot push this social diagnosis aside as irrelevant to educational processes since much of European and American pedagogy, its forms and its methods has contributed to the isolation of western men and women. A decade ago an American thinker, Martin Bloy, put his finger on this:[2]

> From Weber's *Protestant Ethic* to Riesman's *Lonely Crowd*, sensitive cultural analysts have been appalled by the loneliness, the profound spiritual isolation of Western man. Our cultural norms (e.g. the self-made man) and social structures (e.g. the multi-university) have incarnated and deepened that isolation.

Knowledge has not been for sharing but for furnishing a weapon of power in the competitive struggle for the individual. Its edges are sharp and its uses self-centred.

It is the recognition of this flaw in a higher education too much conformed to the pressures of the competitive society which leads directly to the new purpose and role which academics must seek. This is the nourishing of a different sort of vitality, in many ways the opposite of the vitality stimulated by competition. Bloy expresses this new and vital purpose to combat 'spiritual isolation' in terms of destroying dichotomies, between individualism and community, between academia and the world outside, between thought and commitment to action, between mind and body, between material and spiritual. The edges of the academic community, he says, must be blurred to provide a more capacious experience of human community.

Blurring edges between academia and the community at large is a wide-ranging aim. To focus it in a more practical context we will first consider facility in language as a paramount social need in the breaking down of barriers. Language can be the crucial instrument both of self-knowledge and of communication, a powerful means of relatedness in society. William Bouwsma expressed this admirably:[3]

> For if man . . . is 'an animal suspended in webs of significance he himself has spun', he spins these webs primarily from – or with the help of – language. Through language man orders the chaos of data impinging on his sensorium from, in a singularly mysterious and problematic sense, 'out there', organising them into categories and so making them intelligible for himself, manageable, communicable, and therefore socially useful as well as essential to his private adaptation to the world. Indeed, as the humanists of the Renaissance maintained . . . language is the basis of society.

But here we meet a paradox. David Jenkins, reflecting on man as 'a language-using animal', has written: 'Language is a barrier to communication and an instrument of domination', but, almost in the same breath: 'It is by the use of language that men have the chance of creating . . . the richness of a diversity of community and common living.'[4] On the one hand, language is an instrument of power. It has been one of the means by which, in the past, those in power have dominated the inarticulate masses. Dickens bitterly caricatures this in *Hard Times*, in the interview between Mr Bounderby and Stephen Blackpool. On the other hand, through language human beings share some of their deepest perceptions and feelings.

Aspiring towards a truly free society, we now urgently need to turn this two-edged instrument of language towards its use for real communication instead of domination. The ordinary 'layman' needs and must be helped to claim a facility with language which will enable him to meet academics and intellectuals more equally in the give and take of democratic institutions. Those whose main business in life is handling words must be made more conscious of the advantages in debate which this gives them. One has seen local council meetings, for instance, improperly dominated by those to whom talking and writing came easily. Educators at all levels need to be alert to use their powers of articulation not to dominate, but to liberate as many as possible into the freedom of genuine communication.

Above all, the layman needs a defence against demagogues of all colours, that is, against the propaganda power of words. Ever since the ancient masters taught the art of rhetoric the propaganda game with the power of words has always been played by a few, but today the inventions of mass communication have opened the flood-gates to a tide of rhetoric in which words are mishaped into any meanings desired. If any could be called the guardians of words in their exact meanings it should be the academic communities, with their inbuilt obligations to set down the truth, as far as possible, with care and precision, to expose logical fallacies and the use of emotional overtones. Perhaps the academic responsibility is not so much to teach the senators wisdom as to arm the people against the senators' propaganda. Implicit in the idea of a democracy is the undertaking that every person should be helped to reach the highest possible level of individual articulateness of which he is capable. This means practice in using the language tool for himself and a 'space' in which to become responsible for the articulation of his own thoughts and feelings. These could be the gifts of higher education to many more citizens than at present.

But is not this emphasis on words out of date? One of the crucial questions today is the status of verbal language in the civilization of the future. Are not the alternative languages of science and the visual aids of the mass media taking over? Academics whose world is that of the printed word can now be the illiterates in these other languages compared with those who cannot write a grammatical sentence but play computer games with ease. Is verbal language, then, losing its universal position? Maybe, but the case for words as a continuing means of social communication remains strong. We still do the business of democracy, both local and central, with this tool. The reason may lie in its unique capacity to carry both rational and emotional meaning at the same time. If it is agreed that a civilized society needs to be able to express precise relationships of thought in ordered grammatical structures, and further, that it must be able to distil its experiences into generalized concepts, then verbal language, refined and polished for these purposes over so many centuries, must remain the chief means of communication. It is essential, therefore that as many as possible should learn to handle this tool with an understanding of its proper use, with full articulateness and with alertness to the warning signals when it is being improperly used. Philosophy, in the sense of 'getting a clear view of what we are saying' should become an educational medium for the many, since 'the attempt to rise above our muddles and confusions is worthwhile as a contribution to civilisation'.[5] This liberation in the use of language must be one of the targets in higher education for the many.

In his second statement David Jenkins speaks of language as a source of richness and creativity in the community. It is for sharing experience. And here we use the word 'language' in a wider sense. It is significant, for instance, that so often the young find their 'speech' in many other media than words and that when they do use words they often want to burst the rules of grammar and spelling and beat this verbal language into a less rational shape. Analytical methods, with their sharp razor edges, can have a disastrously reductionist effect on words, so that they shrivel and harden, losing all the resonances which ring bells in the imagination. Barbara Reynolds, in a paper on 'Reductionism in Literary Theory', defends the 'speech' of a writer as existing in its own right against the critics who argue that it is 'nothing but' what the reader chooses to make of it. She proclaims the real existence of a piece of creative writing, first as an idea in the mind, then actualized in words and finally demonstrating 'the reality of its potentiality' in the mind and emotions of another.[6] This is genuine communication which may even spark off a creation by that other. But the reductionist handling of word-language sends many young people (and older too) off to those other languages of music, visual art, dance and so forth. These, of course, exist in their own right and play an increasing part in the sharing of experience. They are fundamentally important languages in any civilization and so any drive in our higher education to unstop the springs of communication in our society must embrace programmes in both artistic and verbal languages.

In any such programmes there are tensions to be held: between clarity and mystery, between the cognitive and the affective, between discipline and ecstasy, between individual perception and group emotion. On the one hand, we recognize the need for clear, precise communication, seeking to express exactly the nature of the subject or idea; on the other hand, the mysteries, the complexities, the passions, the beauties of many great themes can never be cut down to size. In great literature clarity and mystery blend in a magnificent creation, as in St Paul's grand discourse on victory over Death in I Corinthians 15, where a tightly-knit logical argument is married to the sense of solemn mystery and exaltation of faith which resounds through the whole passage. 'Connectedness' needs to be a sharing of the mind as well as of the feelings, the communication of full persons, not the animal noises of a mindless group. So discipline remains the tough strand in any true language of persons and the important point here is that learning a discipline is focused in the individual mind, even when the activity is a group one. The ecstasy of singing in the Hymn of Joy of Beethoven's Ninth Symphony depends on the previous concentration of each individual on the part to be learnt.

There is, indeed, a crucial counterpoint to be maintained between together-ness and separateness, and the academic community of learning has, I believe, a unique contribution to make to the understanding of this aspect of community living. It is the purpose of aloneness that is least understood today, for aloneness is not the same as isolation. Every person has a need to sort out and evaluate his/her multitudinous experiences and to reflect within the citadel of the soul on the total meaning of things and of the *I* in their midst. And then each person needs to find the personal language through which to share this meaning with others. But, it may be objected, is self-awareness an experience which the many want? Let the few who will, it can be argued, meditate in solitude, but do not try to bring the many to this daunting moment of self-knowledge in aloneness. A state of undifferentiated 'belonging' in a woolly confusion of mind gives more security than risking estrangement through sharp thought. Let the masses enjoy an undistinguishing comfort while the few sharpen their awareness to the point of discomfort.

We cannot leave it at that. The mysterious imperative to share our experi-ences which is of the very essence of human living demands that we do so at the highest possible level of individual articulation. In the young prize-winner, Christopher Nolan, we have lately seen a moving example of the human spirit bursting out of imprisoned isolation to communicate at a level of high articula-tion (and we may note that his key to freedom was the gift of technology).[7] To help people to be articulate is to help them to be fully human. So 'to put a ring round the individual person' from time to time is not banishment into isolation but a chance for withdrawal in order to connect oneself more fully and clearly with other persons. Thus the cycle is completed: from involvement with that which is outside to the analysis and ordering of experience within, to a further and more articulate relatedness. A rhythm between relatedness and a fruitful solitude is greatly needed in our educational progresses and procedures, but too few people perceive this. A clear modification, in some cases a revolution, in academic attitudes is needed to bring this human rhythm into full educational focus.

There is a close connection between this rhythm and the struggle to find a freshly-minted personal language. There is a debased currency of cliché-jargon in circulation and it is for teachers to attempt that impossibility in economics of making good currency drive out bad. If we can show people how to throw away the tired old phrases and coin a language straight out of an inner personal involvement, we can help them to develop a medium for shared experience which expresses both reasoned understanding and personal emotion. This, in its turn, can sometimes grow into a poetic or artistic language where overtones are more important than rules and the creation bursts out of the model. The use of language runs the whole gamut from the cliché formulations that are useful in a limited sense because they save time, through to the ambiguities and paradoxes in which poets and artists sometimes express their sense of insoluble mystery. But in the educational process itself the emphasis should surely be on the use of language at the point where training in precise, reasoned exposition intersects with the expression of personal excitement and involvement.

So we may set the experience of discovering a richer range of possibilities in using language as one of our aims in widening opportunities in adult education. Closely connected is the second experience of 'open encounter'. Even more than for the young this experience is crucial for mature students, for open encounter is the very foundation of fruitful community relationships. There is a passionate reasonableness which is the key-note of real encounter between mature persons, starting from the intention to recognize 'difference' and listen to it, carried forward through willingness to expose one's own beliefs and judgements to critical scrutiny and issuing, at its best, in greater mutual understanding and sometimes in fruitful modifications of outlook. We desperately need that real dialogue at all levels – in politics, in religion, in ethical problems. It is through wrestling with the barriers of language that estrangements can be transformed into relatedness. Breaking down 'the middle wall of partition' (Ephesians 2:14) is a true function of human discourse, for when human voices prostitute language to the chanting of slogans, a wall of opposition is raised as terrifying spiritually as a row of guns is physically.

It is obvious that in British society today we are confronted by a relatively new 'wall of partition' in race relations. More than a decade ago a magnificent 'essay' in understanding across the black/white divide was made by Margaret Mead and James Baldwin in a seven-and-a-half hour conversation which was taped and published under the title *A Rap for Race*.[8] Here, wrestling with many-tangled knots of emotion mixed with thought, the two conversationalists sought to 'encounter' each other as fully as possible, to bridge the gap of communication, if not wholly of understanding. Commenting on this marathon conversation, John Lawrence said: 'Intuition comes before reason in such matters, but reason must then be used on the insights provided by intuition'.[9] This is surely a text for community education in real dialogue. We need to spend more time and effort to get opposed or disrelated groups wrestling with language in such a way that their intuitively and passionately held beliefs and attitudes are expressed in words that begin to make sense to alien ears, and then in turn using their ears to absorb, by a blend of imagination and reason, what had been unpalatable to them. Genuine speech with the alien is a new kind of speech – disturbing, but exhilarating and muscle-building for the personality. To put a new emphasis on such activities might help us to break out of the deadly pattern of like speaking only to like, while hostile groups shout at each other across great chasms.

Seminars, discussions, debates, provide the floor for such education. Whatever the forum, it is essential to seek the right balance between rational discourse and intuitive understanding. In discussing that conversation between Mead and Baldwin one commentator, Edward Braithwaite, remarked that there was no doubt that 'individuals such as Mead . . . feel that the knots would be more quickly cut by blades of rationality. Baldwin is not so sure. A quick and easy solution with Mead's blade is not the answer because, for him, the rational individual is not the "universal". He has come to know himself not only as ego/id, but as part of a surrealist collective experience of a historical group'.[10] Yet Baldwin found the effort to converse most worth-while and concluded: 'But

we have to achieve some kind of vocabulary. I must say I think we've begun it
. . . to translate for each other and then for many others'.[11] Our western method
of sorting out differences through clear logical processes and sharp distinctions
is so ingrained that it is hard to contemplate any other mode of discourse. Yet an
African palaver can arrive at a common mind without appearing to pass
through a logical sequence of argument and we should not forget that in our own
culture an older and less individualistic society knew how to arrive at wisdom by
collective reflection rather than through one-by-one argument. The Quaker
'sense of the meeting' still overleaps explicit reasoning. Recognition of these
other modes does not detract from the function of higher education to train in
precise, step-by-step discourse, but we should keep clearly before us two things:
that the sharpness of a dividing exercise should ultimately seek to serve the
purpose of reconciliation, not division; that other modes of arriving at common
wisdom are valid and powerful.

   Good communication is central to the health both of individual persons and
of a democratic society. But language is also the gateway to so much else. So a
third experience which is in the gift of higher education to the many is one which
has been called 'growing through books' – if the word 'book' may be extended to
cover the languages of art and music as well as words. It is through the magical
quality of great literature and the arts, as well as history, that the thoughts and
emotions of other people, past and present, resonate in our imaginations and
light up the understanding of our own experience. Here memory is the great
transmitter of innumerable riches which we may gather together in the title of
Proust's tremendous evocation of past experience, *A La Recherche Du Temps
Perdu*. Evoking or transmitting the past needs to be a continuing process of
education since there are many parts of it which pass the young by until
suddenly illuminated by a piece of personal experience. Here it is the marrying
of experience to the past or to an evocative passage in literature which can
become so suddenly and mysteriously illuminating. In 1951 Sir Richard
Livingstone published a prophetic little book on *The Future in Education* in which
he argued cogently for the 'cross-fertilization of theory and experience', using
this as a basis for his campaign for continuing adult education. His preface to a
second impression quotes an example of literature coming alive through
experience which had been sent to him as an illustration of his argument.[12] The
point is dramatically made. Some sixth-formers at school during the War were
studying Macbeth, 'politely interested in a rather detached way, but somewhat
sleepy as a result of nights badly disturbed by (air) raids . . . the atmosphere was
literally revitalized when we came to the following lines:

> The night has been unruly; where we lay
> Our chimneys were blown down; and, as they say,
> Lamentings heard i' the air, strange screams of death;
> . . . the obscure bird
> Clamour'd the livelong night; . . .'

The uses of the past, however, go far deeper than the stimulus of particular
aptnesses or relevances. We need to enlarge our whole vision of the heights and

depths in human beings. So 'growing through books' constitutes our entry into the vast world of human achievement and failure, of nobility and evil, of comedy and tragedy. Dietrich Bonhoeffer – finally executed for his part in an anti-Hitler plot – wrote prophetically of a pervading inability to react to the depths of wickedness in the villain and the flashing brilliance of the saint. There is a crippling superficiality of vision for which the remedy lies surely in opening up the past with the enthusiasm and imagination which may lure many more into encounter with its heroic and poignant dramas. Here is no case for a gentle antiquarian pursuit ('pleasure of ruins' in Rose Macaulay's phrase), but for a study of literature, history or the arts which knocks the mind and revitalises experience for present living.[13]

Another aspect of our need for the past is demonstrated in the extraordinary proliferation today of local history societies, family history societies, folk-lore societies. Amateurs will enthusiastically listen to experts but they also want to dig up their own past. So county archives are invaded by a wide range of people, coach-loads go up to Somerset House to grub up genealogies, extensive family trees are lovingly constructed, folk customs are recorded and collected. The social significance of all this activity hardly needs to be underlined. In an age of mobility and restlessness people discover that they are living in a kind of two-dimensional card-board world. The third dimension of their personal past is missing. It is starvation of the memory that sends people in search of nourishment from family and local history. All these activities need to be 'serviced' in many different ways by the cooperation of professionals with amateurs.

Beyond this particular range of interests, there is exhilarating evidence which one meets in all kinds of people of a wider drive to start an exploration in an area right outside their vocational competence. It is an urge which seems to be a blend of a new curiosity and desire to become articulate in a wider field. This is a pointer to potential demand in the future. Two fostering conditions are already appearing: the rising level of general knowledge due to education through the media and the increasing prospects for leisure. So I have come across a redundant chemist happily researching in medieval Hebrew, a house-wife translating Italian poetry, a retired bank-manager exploring aesthetics, an ex-butler writing a lengthy and well-documented piece of research on a social experiment of the thirties, a group of mentally handicapped people producing their own book of poems. A one-time hippie, going east for inspiration, has transformed himself into an authority on Thibetan civilization. First novels appear from the most unlikely quarters. My examples are perforce taken from the humanities but obviously could be matched many times by those who are drawn to explore the world of natural phenomena. While many adult educational needs call for generous facilities in the form of classes and lectures, these spontaneous individual activities need rather the help of personal advisers. There is a splendid chance for the academic to help bring to a satisfying conclusion projects embraced so enthusiastically by amateurs. This is essentially an 'enabling' role, whether one is correcting syntax, helping to clarify the argument, raising questions or testing conclusions. Many more academic teachers could develop relationships which encourage amateurs to seek their advice. This takes time but in the last analysis it is as rewarding to help other human achievements come to fruition as to see one's own work published.

So we return to the pursuit of curiosity, to Polanyi's 'personal knowledge'. Desire to know, as we have argued, is not the preserve of academics: it is a drive which is shared by many 'laymen' and which can play a large part in building the sense of personal fulfilment which is one source of personal happiness. We undervalue its importance and seriousness when we lump all the multifarious ways in which amateurs pursue their individual enthusiasms as 'hobbies'. There is a patronizing tone in the way we dismiss a hobby as some activity like knitting which passes leisure time pleasantly, or some amateur dabbling in scientific experiments just for fun. Many people have a much more serious passion to know or to construct. They make strenuous efforts to overcome handicaps – lack of time, equipment, professional training – and can become astonishingly expert in their own right. There has for long been this layman– expert strand in our culture. We have prized it far too little. These have been men (and women) of great intellectual curiosity and energy of mind who have also often been people of wide humanity and public service. We think of William Carey, the cobbler with a mission to India, who made a distinguished contri- bution to the study of Indian language, culture and natural history. Joseph Gutteridge, a nineteenth-century ribbon weaver in Coventry, made a unique collection of plants and fossils and also experimented in electricity and in making violins. A third example comes from the 1920s when Simeon Hardwick, a railway man in Darlington, besides being a leading trade unionist, Labour Party chairman, Methodist class-leader and lots of other things, used to lecture on 'wasps, beetles, ants, spiders, butterflies and moths'.[14] These men were the salt of the earth but often unrecognized. We have set too sharp a dividing line between the professional and the amateur. Now higher education institutions could offer a marvellous opportunity to bring these two close together. So, besides a generous provision of courses and facilities offered by the Open University or in local colleges and classes to widen and enrich personal knowledge, we need to bring together the expert and the amateur on a one-to-one basis in a work of serious research. The contributions from the academic side will be training in special skills and the introduction of abstract conceptions or wider contexts which will illumine the particular. What is envisaged here is a kind of net-work of advisory services surrounding each institution of higher education – like a spider's web with happier connotations. 'Doing one's own thing' in this way can be, we have argued, a vital element in personal fulfilment and therefore a contribution to a happier society. There is a crying need to open up our educational resources in order that this flame of personal enthusiasm should be fed.

But there is another and a tougher challenge coming to us as well. In a recent lecture on 'the Underlass and the Future of Britain', Professor Ralf Dahren- dorf not only analyses the sickness of the real underclass but also diagnoses the ills of those who, for one reason or another, are drifting downwards into it.[15] These are not the kind of takers – the willing horses coming to drink at educational fountains – that we have been envisaging, but 'there is a moral case for not dropping any human being, and it is strong', says Dahrendorf.[16] He states emphatically that education is the single most forceful factor in getting people out of such a condition. 'If one can somehow move people ahead in educational terms . . . the probability is high that they will find a way to stand on their own feet.'[17] That 'somehow' constitutes the hard core of the problem. An educational break-through for the most deprived adults seems an impossible miracle. But miracles do happen, given the right 'spark'. The inner-city situation calls desperately for community teachers of genius with just that spark. More immediately possible, perhaps, is the task of arresting the downward drift by vigorous campaigns to lure as many as may be into educational opportunities that really meet their needs. But Dahrendorf warns that educational institutions tend to be part of the official majority establishment and, like other parts of the successful society, they become guardians of the fortress of the majority, shutting their gates on less fortunate minorities. Here is a challenge which cannot be ignored. It needs a particularly sensitive approach to catch the imaginations and stiffen the will to effort of those whose interest in any kind of a 'doing' is steadily shrinking. Here is a situation demanding much faith and a determination to see that the gates of continuing education do not exclude anyone.

Alas – in terms of structures and resources all this seems an impossible demand at this time of economic retrenchment in higher and continuing education. But in the long view the creation of a larger proportion in our society of alert, enterprising, enthusiastic citizens, together with the rescue of as many as possible from a deadly drift into passive acceptance of deprivation, would be an incalculable social benefit, as well as a 'good' in its own right. When will the connection between personal fulfilment and social health be recognized by our rulers?

More competence in skills, a greater articulateness to bring people out of isolation into community, a richer enjoyment of the past, a wider fulfilment of personal interests, more satisfying outlets for creativity – these are some of the gifts which the educational community should be giving back to the society which sustains it. Our economic needs, our standard of living, our general level of education all point to a sharing of learning in higher education on a much wider scale. 'If knowledge is worth while, as many as possible should have it.'[18]

Finally, there is an important caveat to be added. We have already spoken of the double rhythm in personal development – the need for involvement but equally the need for withdrawal. There is a sense which haunts human-beings of 'belonging', yet not belonging. Community learning can be too cosy and containing, and we must ask ourselves: Do we give enough educational 'space' to the loner, the dissident? The Bible gives us a model of two cities – the here-and-now city which seems to engage people fully (Jeremiah tells the exiled Hebrews in Babylon to build houses, plant gardens and seek the peace of the city) [Jeremiah 29:5–7], and that other 'city' towards which there is a perpetual pilgrimage: 'For they declare plainly that they seek a city which hath foundations' (Hebrews 11:14). We have always to allow for the operation of the questioning and critical mind and the far vision which drives the spirit forth on pilgrimage. We must cherish in our midst the particular role of the dissident, the recluse, the nonconformist. We seek a community which makes space available to support some who are prepared to risk irrelevance in the pursuit of an idea, a vision or a hunch.

7

Theological Roots

For Thine is the Kingdom, the Power and the Glory.

Truth has two attributes – beauty and power.
John Henry Newman

I

The Man-right to power is an indisputable claim in the western world today. Yet American pioneers met a very different attitude towards the natural order in the Red Indians they dispossessed as they pushed relentlessly forward. In the endeavour to understand Man's place in creation Jewish imagination framed the great justifying myth of Adam and the animals. It is embodied in a few pregnant sentences at the beginning of the book of Genesis:

> And God said, Let us make man in our image, after our likeness; and let them have dominion over the fish of the sea, and over the fowl of the air, and over the cattle, and over all the earth, and over every creeping thing that creepeth upon the earth. . . . And out of the ground the Lord God formed every beast of the field and every fowl of the air; and brought them unto Adam to see what he would call them; and whatsoever Adam called every living creature that was the name thereof.
>
> (Genesis, i:26; ii:19)

Thus the myth establishes Man's relationship to his environment as one of power *over* it. Perhaps it has only been in Western European soil, however, that the seeds contained in this myth have sprouted so prodigiously. The East has a more relaxed attitude. Lynn White, the historian of medieval technology, contrasted (in a conversation) the attitudes of the Eastern Orthodox and the Western Churches to this Adam story:

> I would like to do a little article on Man's Dominion as it is reflected in Christian iconography. . . . In the Greek manuscripts pertaining to Man's Dominion the pictures show Adam sitting in the garden of Eden quite passively with the animals scattered around him. Sometimes in these Greek paintings the hand of God appears from a cloud to bless the whole situation. The western pictures are very different in mood. God is standing with Adam and he has seized Adam's arm in his left hand. With a very hortatory gesture God is telling Adam exactly what should be done, now.

There is an urgency about this which is totally lacking in the Greek pictures, and the poor animals are far from being relaxed. They are all huddled off in a corner looking scared – and in view of the long-term impact of the attitude reflected in these pictures, I think they have a right to look scared.

It is only in the Renaissance period, however, that the right to dominion begins to come to fruition in scientific enquiry and the exploration of the globe. Sir Francis Drake begins his *Voyage about the World* by an appeal to the mandate of Genesis:[1]

Ever since Almighty God commanded Adam to subdue the earth, there have not wanted in all ages heroicall spirits which, in obedience to that high mandate . . . have expended their wealth, imployed their time, and adventured their persons, to finde out the true circuit thereof.

From this impulse sprang the great flowering of western technology, and today western civilization seems to be based largely on mastery of the natural world.

A significant point in the myth is that Adam is constituted as the 'one who names', endowing the creatures, so it seems, with their very identity. This is a supreme symbol of power. The act of naming is the culminating stage in a process of mastery. One divides, separates out and categorizes by distinguishing characteristics. Finally, the distinguisher gives a name to that which he has identified. He has imposed a set of distinctions on the material, creating separations where none were before and 'fixing' them by his new vocabulary. An undivided world has been divided by the will of a master mind.

The connection between naming and power is well-known in primitive societies. To confer a name gives clear mastery; even to be in possession of a person's name may lead to the exercise of sinister influences. The point is high-lighted for us in the Jewish custom which forbade the sacred name of God to be pronounced. God could not put Himself in the grasp of Man by revealing His Name. When Moses asks what he is to say to the Israelites when they ask who has sent him, God replies: 'I AM THAT I AM. Thus shalt thou say . . . I AM hath sent me unto you' (Exodus 3:4). When Jacob asks the name of the Unknown with whom he had wrestled, he gets a new name himself and a blessing, but no answer to his question.

Today naming signalizes every advance in knowledge. Laboratories spawn new substances, biologists discover new species, new diseases and new drugs. An astronomer, identifying and naming a new heavenly body almost seems to have created it. The processes of analysing and naming become a single act. 'Language', says Cassirer, 'is a determinant in the process of knowing. The act of naming is the indispensable first step and condition of that act of determination which constitutes the task peculiar to pure science'.[2] Our assumption of dominion, is, indeed, such that we often behave as if, before we knew it, something did not exist. The independent existence of the universe around us is denied. There is a simple little story about a child who, by contrast, perceives reality. Someone asks her what her dog's name is. She thinks a moment and then replies carefully: 'Well, *we* call him Patch, but of course I don't know what his *real* name is'. Perhaps it takes a child to recognize that the animals had an independent reality before Adam named them.

The power to name has been singled out as the crucial symbol of a dominating élite by Paulo Freire, the exponent of a revolutionary pedagogy in Latin America. His answer to it is to claim for *all* men the right to 'call the world by its name'. This, he believes, is the basis of a liberal education: 'the naming of the world in reflection and its alteration in action are inseparable for a liberating education'. The striking points in his educational theory are, on one side, an emphasis on naming as domination, so that to break the domination of the few, the many have to be liberated first in their minds through power over vocabulary. Yet, on the other side, there is a recognition that the power of the new society must be based on love, not arrogance, on response to wholes before analysis of parts:[3]

> Calling things by their names involves a claim to domination. The one who calls things – relations, necessities – by new, i.e. actual names is master of the situation . . . At the same time he denies old forms of domination. If a society is organised in such a way that everyone can take part in the procedure of calling things by their names, i.e. judge a situation critically, then it has reached the state of the cultural revolution. But this can only happen when everyone has reached an appropriate faculty of speech – when people have come of age.

Freire's is a revised form of the Adam role. It is the liberation of oppressed people that absorbs his attention and for them he claims the vocabulary of domination. Yet he also speaks of calling things by their *proper* names and in his pedagogy there is clearly a phase of intuitive understanding *before* the power to master enters in:

> The naming of the world is an act of creation and new creation is impossible where these proceedings are not inspired by love. Love is at the same time the foundation of the dialogue and the dialogue itself. If I don't love the world, if I don't love life, I can't enter the dialogue. . . . There is no dialogue without humility. The naming of the world in which people keep on trying to create the world anew, cannot take place as an act of arrogance.

To be articulate, to give dumb experience a voice and language must, to some degree, set man apart from and over against his world, and this is, as Freire claims, part of the liberating experience. Yet, paradoxically, man has also to find the bond which binds him to the real and 'other' world of things and animals as well as people. The 'word' he speaks must be a salutation of separate reality which is itself struggling to be known. From anthropologists we learn how primitive people, even when killing to live, acknowledge the right to *be* in the creatures around them. Red Indians condemn the attitude of the white man: 'How can the spirit of the earth like the white man? . . . Everywhere the white man has touched it, it is sore.'[4] Walking through the countryside as a thinking animal, I sometimes awaken with a start to the vivid life of playing birds and busy insects going on all around, from which I had been totally abstracted and therefore alienated. Have we put ourselves irretrievably outside all this? Can most of us no longer hold:[5]

> . . . unconscious intercourse with beauty
> Old as creation, drinking in a pure
> Organic pleasure . . . ?

Is it not possible now to accept Blake's invitation: 'I'll sing to you to this soft lute and shew you all alive, the World, when every particle of dust breathes for its joy?'[6]

The question, then, is whether increasingly capacity for analysis, articulation and mastery must inevitably alienate human-beings further and further from the natural world they inhabit and, indeed, from each other too, until – in the last extreme – the individual is alone in a wilderness of tools in which nothing has any separate reality outside himself and his urge to dominate. The opposite view – that the liberation of man is bound up with the meaning of the whole creation – was long ago expressed by St Paul: 'For we know that the whole creation groaneth and travaileth in pain together until now. And not only they, but ourselves also . . .' (Romans, 8:22, 23). Within the very Judeo–Christian tradition itself we find the reverse of the Adam-myth in God's concern for all his creatures: 'These wait all upon thee; that thou mayest give them their meat in due season'. Jonah is shown God's concern, not only for the people of Nineveh, but also for its cattle. Job is made to reflect on God's terrible and wonderful works in Behemoth and Leviathan whom he cannot master. (Job, 40.41).

The Hebrew word to know, *yada*, carries the connotation of 'having experience', as well as understanding with the mind. Knowledge to the Hebrew involved, not so much that which could be grasped by reason, as that which made an impact on the whole self. The 'really real' could only be encountered through active participation in history, through engagement in the here and now. This view of knowledge can be placed in contrast to the Greek concept of *logos* which carried the implication of a rational, orderly universe where a word could be attached to a thing, so that man, with his capacity to name the objects of his experience, stood over against a world which could be appropriated in rational terms. Our Hebrew–Greek inheritance endows us with two ways of relating ourselves to our world, two ways of 'knowing': we can be both masters and fellow creatures.

So there is a fine balance to be sought in the use of power between the separateness of domination and the relatedness of communion. The true secret of this balance lies in the recognition of God as Creator. From this the creatureliness of all human-beings follows. We are bound together in an inescapable dependence upon our world and its Maker. Medieval men – wrestling with a burgeoning technology – recognized this when they pictured God as the supreme craftsman moulding the raw materials with his tools, or bending over it to measure the earth with a pair of dividers. Man, too, was a craftsman, made in God's image, but only able to fashion things in obedience to God's laws. In the intoxication of achievement beyond the wildest fancies of medieval men, most people today find this notion of creatureliness repugnant. They wish to acknowledge no source of power other than man's independent genius and effort. There is a story that when Broadcasting House was being built, Sir John Reith, the Director, proposed a dominating inscription in the reception hall: 'The earth is the Lord's and the fullness thereof' (Psalm, 24:1). This suggestion was strongly opposed. The members of the Council dispersed for the summer. When they returned, the inscription flaunted itself before them. It remains a defiant affirmation of a truth that most people are unwilling to acknowledge.

Yet fears for the destruction of our treasure-house world are at least driving the conservationists to recognize that the natural world has laws of its own, even if they do not acknowledge a creator who made those laws. Power is only legitimate when it is exercised under discipline, that is, with recognition that all material things, all creatures, all human-beings, exist through their own laws and to violate these brings destruction on everyone. Naked power, exercised without limitation, in the end not only creates a desert around it, but destroys the exerciser too. Timur (Tamberline) stands in history as a dramatic symbol of the supreme egoist who created a vast desert and collapsed in the midst of triumph. There is an increasing recognition that fundamental laws of being do exist in the universe and that to flout them can bring disaster on a world scale, but too few people face the question: By what sanction do these laws operate? Laws imply a law-giver. The concept of natural law has offered a too easy get-out for those who cannot accept a universal law-giver and wish to base their confidence on the self-sufficiency of Man. The debate goes on: it is age-old; it is always new. Job – with his self-confidence in ruins – questioned omnipotent power and God threw the debate back on him in a series of questions that demanded an answer:

> Who is this that darkeneth counsel by words without knowledge? Gird up thy loins like a man; for I will demand of thee, and answer thou me. Where wast thou when I laid the foundations of the earth? declare, if thou hast understanding. Who hath laid out the measures thereof, if thou knowest? or who hath stretched the line upon it? . . . Or who shut up the sea with doors, when it brake forth . . . And said, Hitherto shalt thou come, but no further: and here shall thy proud waves be stayed? . . . Canst thou bind the sweet influences of Pleiades, or loose the bands of Orion? . . . (Job, 38)

And so on through several magnificent chapters.

II

The classic academic statement of purpose has always been 'the pursuit of truth'. But why, as explorers of knowledge, do we recognize an inward compulsion to establish 'the truth', that is, the objective reality which we are investigating? What restrains us from building fantasies, or fashioning knowledge into forms which suit our ego-centric purposes or the propaganda we wish to make? There are, of course, prudential reasons: fear of being found out in fudging the evidence is a strong deterrent. But this is not an adequate answer. The compelling motive is to find out 'what truly is' (in Leopold v Ranke's famous words: *wie es eigentlich gewesen* – what truly existed). This is implicitly an acknowledgement of that limiting 'otherness' we have been considering. Here researcher and teacher both face the same imperative. The standards we apply to ourselves we must present to our students. As we have seen, our relationship here is triangular: teacher and student form a relationship but both are under an imperative to concentrate attention on the third point of the triangle, the subject. 'I also am a man under authority' (Matthew 8:9), said the centurion to Jesus, in a context in which by worldly standards he was assumed to be the superior. The professional academic is required to make a similar acknowledgement – either explicitly or implicitly – to his students. Both stand under the same authority, that of the subject and its 'hardness', that is, its resistant reality, has to discipline them both.

But the question haunts us: is there any common currency today in words like 'Truth'? Are there any common virtues, either in the academic world or outside it? In his book *After Virtue: a study in moral theory*, Alasdair Macintyre characterizes the 'specifically modern self' as 'emotivist' and describes the key characteristic of this emotivist self as its lack of any ultimate criteria: 'Whatever criteria or principles or evaluative allegiances the emotivist self may profess, they are to be construed as expressions of attitudes, preferences and choices which are themselves not governed by criterion, principle or value. . . . But from this it follows that the emotivist self can have no rational history in its transitions from one state of moral commitment to another. . . . It is a self with no given continuities, save those of the body which is its bearer and of memory which to the best of its ability gathers in its past'.[7]

This is a sharply perceptive diagnosis of the discontinuity, the disaffirmation, so widely felt in the present social context. Yet we talk glibly about passing on our cultural and moral heritage and about the transmission of values. Macintyre's diagnosis undercuts many of the things said in this book. If every personal choice is reduced to how one feels at the moment, long-term commitments disappear and with them any criteria for standards of action. 'What do you think about so-and-so's response to that situation?' asks the ever-hopeful teacher. 'I suppose he did what he liked' (with a shrug of indifference) is the reply which forecloses any attempt at assessment or judgement. This is the mask worn by so many today. The reductionist stance of Macintyre's emotivism is indeed widespread, but, as he says, bits and pieces of an older moral tradition hang around and in surprising situations one stumbles on a deeper, though often muddled, response which acknowledges a standard of what is 'good' and what is 'bad'.

Where do these vestiges of a shared morality come from? Macintyre traces a fascinating history of different societies which were held together by a common tradition of virtue and he draws his clues as to how we might begin to build up a new core concept of the virtues from this history. He notes the great importance in various societies of participating in what he calls a 'practice':[8]

By a practice I mean any coherent and complex form of socially established cooperative human activity through which 'goods' internal to that
form of activity are realised in the course of trying to achieve those
standards of excellence which are appropriate to and partially definitive
of, that form of activity, with the result that human powers to achieve
excellence and human conceptions of the 'ends' and 'goods' involved are
systematically extended.

Then he points out that a 'practice' involves standards of excellence and
obedience to rules which are imposed from outside by the traditions of the
practice. What is required of the individual is to accept this authority and
'subject my own attitudes, choices, preference, tastes to these standards'.[9]
This picture at once recalls the medieval guild concept, with its aim 'to breed
up masters worthy to succeed us in this craft' – a concept out of which the
medieval 'universitas' was born. Of course medieval guild records are littered
with fines for bad workmanship but the ideal was a qualitative 'good'.
Macintyre distinguishes between 'external goods' that are some individual's
property in a competitive situation where there are losers as well as winners and
'internal' goods which constitute a good for the whole community participating
in the practice.[10] This guild conception, as we have seen, still survives in the
academic community but is under great threat from the kind of emotivist forces
that Macintyre analyses. The shared understanding of excellences which still
lights up discourse between scholars and between scholars and students can be
quickly destroyed by pursuit of career or market 'goods'. Moreover, the
educational function of a true 'practice' is today also threatened in a subtle way
by the growing use of the word 'socialization' to describe it. This word nearly
always carries pejorative overtones, implying that individuals are being man-
ipulated, even 'processed' into becoming conformists. On the contrary, both
Polanyi and Macintyre, while seeing apprenticeship or education in a 'practice'
as a method of passing on what is good, both recognize the element of change, of
conflict, of breaking away, as each generation seeks its own integration of truth.
Polanyi analyses the relationship of systematic apprenticeship to the dynamics
of discovery. The first process ensures that apprentices assimilate for themselves the settled instincts and performative skills which characterize the living
masters of the tradition. The second process ensures that such apprenticeships
do not deteriorate into a benevolent brain-washing, but that the new masters
dedicate their energies to revealing as-yet-undisclosed manifestations of
those realities they serve. The first process ensures the faithful handing down
of the traditions; the second process ensures that the tradition itself is being
periodically renewed.[11]
    The urgency of Macintyre's argument lies in his judgement that society
disintegrates and human life becomes chaotic where there are no shared values
but only individual inclinations of the moment. The recovery of virtue, he
believes, can only be through shared experience which gives a continuity of
meaning to individual lives. Here Macintyre's perception comes close to
Polanyi's emphasis on the need for tacit knowledge and the indwelling of an

intellectual 'home' as a *sine qua non* in education. Macintyre distinguishes three facets of this. The first is the experience of participating in a true practice in which the acquisition of technical skills is transformed and enriched by the common 'internal goods'. The second is the experience of entering into a historical tradition: 'What I am is in key part what I inherit, a specific past related to my present. I find myself part of a history'. But this is no dead hand: 'A living tradition is a historically extended socially embodied argument'. And so the third is a historically extended socially embodied argument'. And so the third experiential element in the pursuit of virtue is the continuity of an individual life, responding to and developing out of the shared inheritance: 'The unity of an individual life consists in the unity of a narrative . . . quest'. The essence of the quest lies in setting one's sights on the long-term pursuit of virtue rather than on the fleeting satisfaction.[12]

This last point in Macintyre's argument chimes with Gabrielle Taylor's analysis of the concept of Integrity. Her approach is by way of 'thinking of the person possessing integrity as being the person who "keeps his inmost self intact", whose life is "of a piece", whose self is whole and integrated. My claim is that it is this view of integrity which is the fundamental one. The person of integrity keeps his self intact and the person who lacks integrity is corrupt in the sense that his self is disintegrated'.[13] This, she points out, is not a static view of the person: he can certainly change, for example through the recognition of mistakes, but 'he cannot change his commitments just when he feels so inclined. He must see a reason for changing them, otherwise he does not count as having been committed at all'.[14] So commitment is one essential element of the integrated person: he is indissolubly linked with his future. He is equally linked with his past: '. . . prominent among the criteria for personal identity are memory conditions . . . that we have experiential memory is essential to being a person at all. . . . There is thus a two-way process which links different experiences to each other and because of which they are all one person's experiences and constitute his life'.[15]

Both Macintyre and Taylor are thinking in the wider social context, but their insights have peculiar relevance to the academic situation. They think in terms of experiences, not intellectual formulations and that is precisely how we should tackle the deep problems of pursuing 'virtue' and 'truth' in our educational institutions. The true academic 'practice' has not yet been destroyed, but its 'internal goods' must be much more explicitly understood and transmitted if they are to survive. They must be openly shared with the next generation of students. Macintyre, in a striking contrast with Nietszche's great Man-in-isolation, emphasizes the necessity of relationships:[16]

For, if the conception of the good has to be expounded in terms of 'practice', of the narrative unity of a human life and of a moral tradition, then goods and with them the only grounds for the authority of laws and virtues, can only be discovered by entering into those relationships which constitute communities whose central bond is a shared vision of and understanding of goods. To cut oneself off from the shared activity in which one had initially to learn obediently as an apprentice learns, to isolate oneself from the communities which find their point and purpose in such activities would be to debar oneself from finding any good outside oneself.

The essential model is that of master/apprentice, not purveyor/consumer. It is through the relationships of shared enthusiasms, of questionings and searchings, of wrestlings for clear thought, of reflectings and concludings, that the excellences of our academic 'practice' can be transmitted, not only to those who will 'succeed us in this craft', but to that much larger throng who may carry the experience of virtue into the wider social context.

Sharing the 'goods' of the practice itself includes historic tradition. A small illustration of the way this works in the university can be seen in the special role which memorial services play, especially in educational institutions, in handing on concepts of virtue. At their best, they are a reflection on a life's experience, usually the life of a scholar and/or teacher. The *pietas* which inspires those who orate and those who attend can be enriched and enlarged by the evocation of a real personality in whom – for all his/her failings – dedication to truth and intellectual integrity shines through. The art of composing such addresses seems to have developed lately and to be taken with great seriousness. Perhaps there is an instinctive sense that endangered traditions can best be defended by bearing witness to the core commitments of a life, even while portraying it 'warts and all'. This is the point at which the whole Judeo–Christian 'practice' becomes relevant, bearing witness, as it does, to the deep rooting of the individual's life in the long history of God's dealings with human-beings and societies. Chanting the Psalms (even though literally they deal with the one small history of Israel) symbolically enfolds the individual person – here today and gone tomorrow – within the timeless (or timelong) reality of God's care which gives meaning to all a person's tiny purposes and commitments. So we say: 'I will remember the works of the Lord: surely I will remember thy wonders of old. I will meditate also upon all thy work, and talk of thy doings' (Psalm 77). The tragedy is that this practice now appears so remote to so many.

Educationally, it is the core commitments of individual lives that ultimately concern us, and in particular the continuing commitment to seek 'the truth'. How do we nurture the 'narrative continuity' of growing persons who are developing, changing, meeting 'differences', embracing new purposes? How do we help them to take their past into themselves and commit themselves to their purposes for the future? We have already in part discussed this. The question to be asked here is where are the roots of commitment to virtue, how deep do they lie? Gabrielle Taylor, analysing the compulsions laid on a person, says: 'There is to the "must" or "cannot" a background consisting of the various implications of some one commitment or of inter-related commitments'.[17] But she does not investigate the root of that over-riding factor, remarking that it is something we cannot catch directly. The argument of this book has been that it is the embracing of a sovereign good that constitutes the root of commitment to virtue. The Christian must then go on to affirm that this perception of sovereign good is the gift of God in whom all true 'goods' are rooted. This is a stance of faith which cannot be imposed on any other person but it means that the search for virtue, for a commitment to the good, is always seen by a Christian – in whomever or whatever guise we meet it – as a search for the kingdom of God. As such it is an infinitely precious search for the pearl of great price.

Thus the ultimate sanction for the academic affirmation that truth must not be tampered with is theological. Because all things derive their being from God the Creator they are sacred. Although we always see through a glass darkly, our knowledge of the world of nature and of man is part of God's self-revelation to us. We learn that 'openness' to the truth brings fulfilment of the promise: 'Ye shall know the truth and the truth shall make you free' (St. John, 8:32). If integrity is conceived of as an integration around a central commitment to truth, then that truth ought to be the most complete and all-embracing in its self-authentication. This Christians find in the truth of God in Christ. It is a liberating truth; it is a uniting truth. The Christian affirmation is that things will *not* fall apart as we learn more; that the Centre *will* hold. The connection between seeking truth and seeking God was explicitly made by David Jenkins in his inaugural lecture at Leeds:

> God is very like Truth in the understanding and vision of scholars. He is worth pursuing, responding to and exploring into at all times – and under all circumstances, good, bad, and indifferent. To seek Him and occasionally to find something of Him is a more than sufficient reward in itself.[18]

Jenkins goes further. He puts his finger on a characteristic of the subject matter of theology which goes to the heart of the scholar's understanding of truth:[19]

> Moreover it is also in the dynamics of the story and theory out of which Theology lives that God is concerned to work through particularities. Thus . . . Theology can be a reinforcement to that perseverance in the study of particularities according to different disciplines which is essential both if truth and scholarship are to be advanced and if there is to be a contribution from our various disciplines . . . to society's requirements for 'making a living'.

Yet, he says, 'Theology is obliged by its interior logic and by the sources of faith and community from which it arises to be concerned with universal claims and fundamental questions'. Here is a model for that fruitful interaction between the particulars which are the meat of daily life in academic institutions and the universals to which, we have argued, we must give time for reflection. And Jenkins leads on from this to suggest that in this combination of the particular and the universal there lies a pointer to the solution of the present worries about the social effectiveness of higher education with which this book began. Christian theology claims:[20]

> to have found an absolutely unique combination of particular events and universal significance in and around the historical personality, Jesus of

Nazareth. It may be therefore that the practice of Theology as a continuing academic discipline can make its own contribution to the re-
assessment which we need of the appropriate set of working relationships
between the claims of long-term scholarship and research and the immediate claims for the deliverance of knowledge, skills and training which
are socially applicable and required. Certainly, if Theology remained
faithful to its own central tradition, it would have to hold that there is no
contradiction between commitment to the immediate and the urgent
response to the ultimate and the transcendent. What is required is
continuing attempts to combine critical re-assessment of practical responses with sustained vision and hope in maintaining a creative balance
and tension.

Theology as an academic study supports the kingdom of truth in which the
true scholar aspires to be a member. In doing so, he puts himself under its
authority but he is also under obligation to share its traditions and the practice
of its virtues with the next generation of seekers.

III

'Sparkles of Glory'[21] inhabit our world. Few would deny this. It is a characteristic human attitude to respond in wonder to the intricacies shown by the
microscope or the vastnesses shown by the telescope, to the heroisms of human
life and death, to the grandeurs of literature, art and music. Glory lies all around
us in academic study. 'Here's glory', said Humpty Dumpty to Alice, but what is
this glory?[22] It transcends definition and can only be described in terms of
revelation, the shining forth of an inner beauty which is made manifest through
an outer form 'What calls forth the ecstatic delight of an Archimedes or a Kepler
is the conviction that their discovery gives them a perception of the nature of
things . . . a true indicator of reality.[23] We should not dismiss Keat's discovery
that 'beauty is truth, truth beauty . . .' as an outworn cliché:[24] it is of fundamental importance. Any 'thing' created by God has its own truth which is in
essence beautiful because it is the expression of a perfect divine thought. (In
parenthesis we may note the use of the word 'thing' as an all-embracing
category for the works of God's creation by, for instance, St Augustine and St
Thomas Aquinas. This use vastly upgrades the word 'thing', making it a symbol
of all creative activity. Indeed, we commonly use it so in the phrase 'doing your
own thing'.) We recognise this truth/beauty through a wholeness of response to
a whole reality in which we acknowledge a largeness or mystery beyond our
grasp. Moses was commanded to take off his shoes before the burning bush:
there is an academic 'taking off of shoes' which we do instinctively, mostly
without recognising what we do. But if it is a revelation, what does it reveal?
Those who fear where that question is leading them draw back at this point.
'Majesty', 'grandeur', 'nobility' and other such value-laden words are expressions that would lead them too far: better to analyse and understand the
parts than to feel and attempt to describe the whole in this ambiguous language.

So a scholar or student can distance himself from an experience of wonder or ecstasy because of its dangerous implications.

Not so our friend Thomas Traherne who, we remember, celebrated the glory all around him. Traherne's sense of delight and felicity could be open and unashamed because he had no doubt about the nature of the universe. It was God's world and therefore it followed inevitably that the source of all glory was God's self-revelation. To Iris Murdoch this attitude is prayer: 'Prayer is properly not petition but simply an attention to God which is a form of love'.[25] The Christian claim is that, whether we recognize it or not, our response to glory is a response to God. For the Christian, the transfiguration of this world is brought to a focus in the transfiguration of the Man Jesus. 'It is good for us to be here' (Matthew 17:4) was Peter's reaction on the Mount of Transfiguration, 'Let us build three tabernacles'. Inhabiting a moment of time which is suffused with wonder and delight is a sojourning in the presence of what D. H. Lawrence calls 'the tent of the Holy Ghost'.[26] We should not hurry either ourselves or our students away from it in a flurry of embarrassment. Of course the descent from the mountain follows with all its consequent disillusionment and failures, but it is the fleeting moment of glory that sparks off our studies.

Why are we thus fired? The secret is that 'delight', 'wonder', 'felicity' are signals of a living relationship. We are here not in the dumb world of tools or the inanimate world of concepts but in a world that speaks to us in its own language. In a recent article Geoffrey Price quotes Einstein, at the age of four, receiving a 'deep and lasting impression' from observing the movement of the compass: 'Something deeply hidden had to be behind things'.[27] Much later Einstein wrote:[28]

> The most beautiful and most profound experience that man can have is the sense of the mysterious. This constitutes the foundation of religion and of all other profound striving in art and science. He who has not experienced it seems to me – if not dead – at least blind . . . It is enough for me to sense these mysteries with astonishment and to attempt in humility to formulate with my mind a scanty representation of the sublime structure of reality.

Reflecting on this experience, Price observes:[29]

> That experience . . . usually lies dormant and hidden in us, restrained by our tendency to seek to organize our perceptions in available conceptual categories. . . . That is not the knowledge of the 'domesticated university', the knowledge gathered for survival, pleasure or power. That is what is learnt by allowing the hidden desire of wonder to rise to consciousness and initiate a movement of the entire personality. . . . the world is encountered not as an extension of the isolated self, but as an independent yet strangely intelligible manifestation of existence.

In her book *Old Arts and New Theology – the beginnings of theology as an academic discipline*, Gillian Evans describes the twelfth-century understanding of *speculatio* as 'gazing on the divine' – a vision or gazing which 'involves contemplation' and 'is, essentially, a devotional exercise'. By contrast, she points out, 'the hard-edged academic exercise of later twelfth-century speculative theology had been stripped of all such elements: it became an activity of the mind in which religious emotion had little or no place. . . . the divorce of contemplation from abstract thought of an academic kind was complete'.[30] That distinction between intellectual thought and contemplation is still valid. Jenkins, in the lecture from which we have already quoted, picking up Evans' point, asks: 'Can theology live with this divorce? But can it live as an academic subject without it? For what has the class-room (? or the laboratory) to do with "devotion" . . . ?'[31] We should widen the question and ask: Can academic study in general live with a sharp divorce between abstract thought and contemplation? Jenkins turns back to a definition of the Greek word *theōria* for guidance: 'spiritual contemplation, not always too sharply distinguished from philosophical contemplation'. While there would be little question that devotional practice is inappropriate in the class-room, we should recognize the blurring of the distinction when reflection or abstract thought passes into gazing in wonder. Jenkins concludes:[32]

> whether one is a believer in God or not, or through whatever religious tradition one explores this, is there not a strong case for keeping an awareness of a dimension of yearning, wonder and desire for commitment to true and lasting value as a necessary part of what it is to be human?

IV

Yet – 'felicity', 'delight', 'wonder' – is it not sheer hypocrisy to pretend that these words belong to higher education? Drudgery, disillusionment, failure are surely the key words. As far as drudgery is concerned, this need present little serious problem: in this context it is just an unpleasant word for discipline. Every long-term joy worth working for involves labour, hard slogging, persistence. 'Who for the joy that was set before him endured the pain' (Hebrew 12:2) is our text. Disillusionment and failure are another matter. The causes of disillusionment are many and complex but the particular one on which I wish to focus attention here can be ascribed bluntly to the sin of academic teachers. It is our failure to communicate the living, personal meaning of knowledge and its creative working (like leaven) in the spirits of all who share in it. In theological terms it is the gift of the Holy Spirit which is lacking. We are blind to the truth that the gift often has to be transmitted through ourselves. Charles Wesley's hymn, though not intended as such, speaks vividly in the academic context:

> O Thou who camest from above
> The pure celestial fire to impart,
> Kindle a flame of sacred love
> On the mean altar of my heart. . . .

> Still let me guard the holy fire,
> And still stir up thy gift in me.

We, the teachers, are called by the Spirit to be stirrers up.
But there will be a barrage of opposition to such an outrageous statement.

Many academic teachers regard it as part of their duty to conceal all emotions. But if Polanyi's concept of personal knowledge is valid, the attempt to conceal one's own involvement is – in general, though there may be exceptions – a misguided and sometimes disastrous academic attitude, as I have tried to show. Cynicism, as distinct from scepticism, is an even more destructive agent to quench the smoking flax of enthusiasm and personal meaning. But even those teachers who do acknowledge their responsibility to communicate personal meaning will mostly react with violent feeling against an idea of connecting their vocation with the Holy Spirit. Well, the Holy Spirit can look after himself. What must be said here with passion is that, of all the gifts the students need from us, *faith in the goodness of knowledge and its creative meaning in our personal lives is paramount.* 'The hungry sheep look up and are not fed' is our greatest indictment.[33]

But failure – that takes us deeper still. In the formal organization it meets students and teachers all the time, in examination and career failure. There are outside factors involved in failure. But inside failures, failures in personal living can poison the springs of motivation and produce the maladjustment, unhappiness and *accidie* which no stimulating and sympathetic teacher can cure with ease. Here we reach a dimension of human living which we all share; the element of tragic failure which interlaces all our experience. How do we respond to student tragedy and to our own?

Dr Stephen Prickett has recently turned our minds towards the significance of failure as an integral part of education. In a memorable essay which analyses the experience of failure in the development of various writers, he argues that personal growth is closely bound up with this experience: 'As Wordsworth and Mill (J.S.) both discovered, it is not the high points of achievement that one looks back upon in retrospect as moments of growth, but periods of doubt, guilt and failure'.[34] Yet English education is focused on success. Sharpening the implications of this insight in a conference summing-up he says:[35]

> . . . one of the fundamental criticisms I would wish to make of liberalism is its lack of capacity to come to terms with failure. If you ask me to define very briefly what I thought the aim of education was, I would go out on a limb and say 'To enable people to come to terms with their own failures'. That is not in fact so far from the view that David Levy was suggesting when he talked about enabling man to come to terms with his limitations and so see himself as a finite creature. Sooner or later everybody comes up against serious problems of personal inadequacies and personal failures. Information is less important than self-knowledge.

So our task is set for us: to enable young people to meet the external failures thrust upon them by society and the internal failures of their own souls. First, they have to come to terms with hard social and economic factors blocking the fulfilment of their desires and ambitions and with the restraints, sometimes tyrannies, thrust upon them by the social bundle in which they are bound. In the category of 'given' limitations are also the limitations of one's own talents and physical strength. Our sensitivity as teachers to all such factors is enormously important. And so often the counselling goes hard. Patience is a gift of the Holy

Spirit but it is perhaps the hardest gift for young people to cultivate. In the world of material things instant satisfaction reigns, so why is patience necessary in spiritual things? The answer lies in what the acceptance of limitation and disappointment can create in the human soul. Acceptance fertilizes if – and it is a big if – married to continuing aspiration and faith in the struggle towards a goal, albeit unseen. We think of Beethoven writing his greatest music in the despair of total deafness. Or of the haunting gaiety of some of the tunes in Mozart's last works, when death was closing in to quench all the tunes left in him. Again, the life of Harold Owen (brother of Wilfred Owen, the poet) shows us the fruits of patience: Harold greatly desired to be a painter but was forced by the pressure of a poor family into the merchant navy, emerging finally as the creator of a remarkable family autobiography.[36]

But we still have to plunge deeper into the meaning of failure. It springs, not only from factors which are imposed upon us, but from our own inner failures of courage, persistence and obedience and from the harbourage we give to those rank weeds of vanity, envy and selfishness. What do we call these failures, if not sins? We will not, however, spend time on the name: it is the recognition of failure in the human intention and will that is crucial. Perhaps the experience which strikes most deeply into the springs of a spurious self-confidence is one which Stephen Prickett has called 'disconfirmation'. One's false confidence or false sense of mastery over one's own destiny is suddenly shattered by confrontation with a real truth, whatever form it may take. There is a classic, and for its period quite astonishing, portrayal of such an experience at the end of Dante's *Purgatorio*. The poet has come through all the experiences of hell and purgatory guided by his master Virgil. He has been frightened and at times chided like a child, but always guided by the rational discourse of his master towards an understanding of man's nature and the conditions for its true fulfilment. Now he stands at the top of the Mount of Purgatory, ready to step forward into the Earthly Paradise. The last time Virgil speaks to him he salutes Dante in the terms of the humanist 'whole man':[37]

> Free, upright and whole, is thy will, and it were
> a fault not to act according to its promptings;
> wherefore I crown and mitre thee over thyself.

Dante goes forward, eager to meet Beatrice and confident in his own understanding. He does, indeed, meet Beatrice but not as he expects: he is instantly thrown from the proud seat of the humanist by the reproaches with which she lashes him and dissolves in bitter weeping. Dante has to come to terms with a much deeper self-knowledge before, cleansed in the waters of Lethe, he can undertake the mission to which Beatrice calls him.

The duality of our nature is a fact that self-examination should make clear to all of us. Anyone who tries to look honestly at him/herself has to say with St Paul: 'For the good that I would that I do not: but the evil which I would not, that I do.' (Romans, 7:19) Even our delights can be tainted, for the sparkles of glory are so often quenched in a miasma of self-conceit. The cry of failure within the soul is a universal experience. It is too often a despairing cry, yet – strangely

– this cry which acknowledges the full depth of evil within can in itself mark the beginning of release. That is why the music which, all down the ages, has expressed this universal conviction of failure, rises to such tremendous heights of grandeur and beauty. The vast *Miserere nobis* of human experiences crashes on our ears as universal tragedy, but the great musicians are telling us that out of the depth hope rises.

The most profound expression of human failure and hope is embodied in the Christian liturgy. It brings together the *Gloria* and the *Agnus Dei*. Liberation from failure, release into new life, is the unlocking of a prison door. Who provides the key? John Bunyan caught exactly the right metaphor in *The Pilgrims Progress*. The pilgrims, locked in the dungeon of Giant Despair, suddenly *saw* the key lying there, waiting to be picked up. The Christian belief is that we do not make our own key to freedom; it is the greatest of the God-given things in human lives, but ours is the choice whether or not to pick it up. So the *Miserere nobis* of the Christian liturgy is not the cry of a drowning man to anyone within earshot to rescue him, but is directed specifically to the God-in-Christ who believes in each one of us and therefore can give us the faith to persist. Thus recognition of the failures we make for ourselves through disobedience to the laws of our being is the beginning of salvation, the opened door of release into new life.

These theological roots are tough and unpalatable to the digestion of many today. It is hard to find an adequate 'language for failure', as Prickett puts it, one that will make sense of these fundamental experiences of self-knowledge and salvation (or liberation). What matters most is that when it falls to any of us to give counsel – whether to students or others – it is our perception of what lies in the depths that must guide our words. Self-deception has to be stripped off and from this death life will be resurrected. Perhaps the teacher must contribute to both experiences, but most importantly must pour out in abundance faith in the individual person, in his/her potentialities for growth and possibilities in the life ahead. There are many different types of loving, appropriate to many different situations. In the context of education it is a special loving of the potential in a person that seems in particular to be called for. The New Testament gives us a text for teachers and students alike: 'It doth not yet appear what we shall be . . .' (John, 3:2) It is this vision which can call forth the supporting love needed. Prickett has pointed out that what brought Mill through his crisis of failure was *the power of human feeling* in Wordsworth's poetry. This is the support students need. A university Registrar, asked what he believed to be the role of a Chaplain, replied, without hesitation 'to tell members of the University that they are loved'.

V

Finally we discover that one answer to these evils of isolation, disconnectedness, fragmentation, alienation lies in an old but newly rediscovered idea – celebration. 'Celebration' carries two important overtones: it is salutation of that which is of intrinsic worth in itself; it is a shared experience of delight, since celebration needs more than one person. Thus celebration is a coming together in praise of 'worth'. In a paper entitled *Celebration* A. M. Allchin reflects on the significance of this phenomenon as a sign of the break-down of something central to our 'tired, strained, over-serious, over-conscious society'. He sees the movement of young people today as a spiritual quest, having in common 'that they seek quality of life rather than quantity, that they are opposed to the cult of efficiency and acquisitiveness, (that they) want to find time to contemplate, to celebrate, and (that they) hope that there is in life something or someone worth contemplating, celebrating'.[38] What is striking in his thought is that he relates the word celebration to the healing of breaches, the uniting of that which was scattered, the bringing together of opposites. In pre-industrial cultures 'people knew more easily what celebration was: something which occurs when opposites come together, when unity is achieved'. Today we need the knitting up of many rents in our torn consciousness and divided societies:[39]

> The opposites which need to come together for a celebration are of many kinds: conscious and unconscious; critical intellect and intuitive intellect; experience of time, experience of eternity; individual and group; personal and social, myself and the world. For celebration the gulf between objective and subjective needs to be bridged. We have to go beyond this cramping distinction, which is so obstructive to our understanding of persons, and find ourselves in a more intimate, co-inherent relationship with others and the world around us. In our culture we are taught to make a sharp division between the self and the world, as if the world stood opposite us 'out there' whether we noticed it or not, and as if the self were an observing consciousness, trapped in a bag of skin.

Allchin sees the drug phenomenon as a desperate means of breaking out of this boxed-up, separate self, existing in a desert of tools. For the first time, some users of drugs report, they are able to look at things outside the perspective of 'usefulness' and to experience the feeling of being one with the universe. As against the technologically oriented man who perceives the world only in so far as it suits his purpose, the drug-taker, as reported by Allchin, 'feels liberated to perceive the world more nearly as artists, mystics and primitive people perceive it; the world is more alive, more personal, more resonant with unity, more terrifying, full of variety, of complexity, and of astonishing surprise. The language of function recedes; the language of being expresses the experience more accurately.'[40] Allchin is not, of course, advocating the use of drugs but pointing up the spiritual starvation which drives people drugwards. He finds this description of drug-experience 'very like the vision of the world seen in the light of God, full of the creative energies of God, . . . what the Greek Fathers called *physike theoria*, or natural contemplation. . . . We are dealing here with a vision of the world as a world in which God is at work, not necessarily or even probably with the direct encounter with God himself'.[41]

Many students today understand and use this language of religious experience through words such as epiphany, liturgy, ritual, even though their applications may be wildly untraditional. Yet, perceiving that the integration of their own inner being is bound up with the restoration of the whole creation, they would understand Allchin when he says: 'It is a sure sign of the wholeness of tradition when both things are held together in one. Creation and redemption, man and nature come together in the celebration of God's goodness'. They would agree that 'joy and thanksgiving are things that grow by being shared' and even respond to the invitation of a seventeenth-century preacher quoted by Allchin: 'Let man become the spokesman of the whole creation. Let all things enter into the dance of praise'.[42]

There is another dimension to this life of connectedness. In a perceptive Third Programme talk on the Russian thinker Fyodorov, Donald Nicholl described the surprisingly contemporary reflections of this nineteenth-century writer on the disrelatedness of the modern world and its remedies. He saw the modern city as 'an aggregate of non-brotherly states', because its raison d'etre was 'to provide human beings with opportunities to seek an advantage over one another'.[43] The world for him was full of disjunctions, in particular, the separation of thought from work, that is, the élite from the masses, and man from nature. But the most striking element in his thought is that cutting ourselves off from our ancestors symbolizes, in a sense, our whole state of disrelatedness. 'A man who would not, if he could, return life to those from whom he received it is not worthy of life or of freedom'.[44] Fyodorov saw the common task of humanity as the resurrection of our forefathers. Whatever he meant by this astonishing statement, his point about the link between our present state of disconnectedness and our disregard for our roots is surely valid for us. 'We are led', says Nicholl, 'to see the truth in Fyodorov's contention that the non-kinship and absence of genuine brotherhood which he noticed with respect to the living is essentially connected to, is matched by, indifference, and what he called a falling-away-from-kinship in regard to the dead'.[45] One could say that persons cut off from connections with their past are 'weightless'. Certainly the desperate search of rootless individuals for personal identity today emphasizes the insecurity of our fragile, fragmented mode of consciousness. Reconnecting ourselves with the living past is a vital part of celebration. This is why Christians celebrate saints days. The vision of Mount Zion with the peoples flowing towards it, towards their fellowship with that multitude which no man could number' (Revelation, 7:9) is one of great power and exaltation. It is the inspiration for all true celebration:

We have drawn near to Mount Zion, to the city of the living
  God, to the heavenly Jerusalem
We have drawn near to the angelic hosts, to a solemn
  feast:
To the assembly of the first-born.
We have drawn near to God who judges the world, to the
  spirits of the righteous made perfect
To Jesus the mediator of a new covenant.
                    (From the Orthodox liturgy for the
                        Feast of St. Gregory of Nyssa.)

Celebration of 'worth', conviviality, the 'communion of saints' these dimensions of human experience run back into their theological roots. 'Where two or three are gathered together in my name . . .' carries a wider meaning than the overtly religious. For everything of true worth manifests the Creator and the celebration of such is truly 'in his name', whether explicitly recognized or not. A generation or two ago there was a custom to read at end of term celebrations in schools St Paul's famous charge to the Philippians:

> Rejoice in the Lord alway; and again I say, Rejoice. Let your moderation be known unto all men. The Lord is at hand. . . . Finally, brethren, whatsoever things are true, whatsoever things are honest, whatsoever things are just, whatsoever things are pure, whatsoever things are lovely, whatsoever things are of good report; if there be any virtue, and if there be any praise, think on these things.
>
> (Philippians 4:4–8)

The profound implications of this passage passed most of the assembly by – it was the holidays that were at hand, not the Lord. But the instinct to put these words in the setting of an educational celebration was sound. The Lord is, indeed, at hand when our hearts glow within us and we share the excitement or the delight or the ecstasy or the memory given to us in the world of knowledge. There are immensely wider and deeper sources of conviviality than beer or champagne.

Nothing less than a radical return to fundamentals will meet what is essentially a crisis of spirituality among teachers in higher education today. In this context Melvyn Matthews has defined spirituality as 'Not simply a religious stance' but rather as being concerned with 'the inner or "hidden" areas of life'. 'Academics . . . should realise that the academic profession is, profoundly, a spiritual profession, a profession which should be pursued at the most profound level of human personality'.[46] To shrink the human person – whether academic or student – down to the hardened substance of a purely mental activity is to deny its reality and make a travesty of learning. Universities and colleges have to be concerned with whole persons. 'Unless the essential connection is made between thinking, feeling and caring, all our so-called thinking is an evasion of thinking. . . . Unless a university commits itself to the creation of an environment where emotional and ethical development command parity of esteem with mental development, it will not nourish the logical thought processes which can alone come to grips with the appalling problems of the contemporary world.'[47]

Notes and References

Chapter 1

1 J. A. Pope, 'The role of universities in a changing technologically based industrial society', *Journal of the Royal Society of Arts*, September 1979, p. 615.
2 *Manchester Newsletter* of the Association of University Teachers, December 1987, précising John Griffith, *The Attack on Higher Education*, The council for Academic Freedom and Democracy, October 1987.
3 Royal Society of Arts (1982) *Recognition Scheme*.
4 Ibid.
5 *The Times*, 31/5/1985.
6 'Oration by the Vice-Chancellor', *Oxford University Gazette*, Supplement to No. 4081, 15 October 1987 (unpaginated).
7 Ibid.
8 Ibid.
9 Ibid.
10 Quoted Drusilla Scott, *Everyman Revived. The Common Sense of Michael Polanyi*, Lewes, Sussex, Scott, The Book Guild, 1985, p. 40.
11 Iris Murdoch, *The Sovereignty of Good*, London, Routledge & Kegan Paul, 1970, p. 66.
12 Martin Buber, *I and Thou*, trs. R. Gregor Smith, Edinburgh, T. & T. Clark, 1937, p. 3.
13 Ibid, p. 11.
14 Sinclair Goodlad (ed.), *Study Service. An examination of community service as a method of study in higher education*, Windsor, NFER, 1982, p. 25.
15 Ibid, p. 30.
16 Michael Polanyi, *The Tacit Dimension*, New York, Doubleday, 1966, p. 25.

Chapter 2

1 Matthew Arnold, 'Empedocles on Etna', *The Poems of Matthew Arnold*, ed. K. Allott, London, Longman, 1965, p. 169.
2 Park Honan, *Matthew Arnold. A Life*, London, Weidenfeld & Nicholson, 1981, pp. 205–7.
3 Matthew Arnold, *Culture and Anarchy. The Complete Prose Works of Matthew Arnold*, ed. R. H. Super, Ann Arbor, University of Michigan Press, 1960–77, V, p. 233.
4 Honan, op. cit., p. 345.
5 Quoted ibid, p. 367.

6 C. S. Lewis, *They asked for a Paper*, London, Bles, 1962, p. 114.
7 Michael Polanyi, *Personal Knowledge, Towards a Post-Critical Philosophy*, London, Routledge & Kegan Paul, 1958, p. 208.
8 John Henry Newman, *An Essay in Aid of A Grammar of Assent*, London, Burns & Oates, 1881, p. 40.
9 Ibid.
10 Ibid.
11 Ibid, p. 75.
12 Scott, op. cit., p. 33. We may note that many detective stories are based on this principle: a set of 'facts' has been arranged, according to accepted rules, in a pattern which points to one conclusion, accepted by most people. But one person notices an oddity in the evidence which does not fit in and the significance of which has escaped everyone else's attention. He/she works on the problem, starting from this clue, until the accepted solution is proved false and a quite different 'true' one emerges.
13 Scott, op. cit., p. 34.
14 Polanyi, *Personal Knowledge*, p. 135.
15 Polanyi, *Tacit Dimension*, pp. 75–6.
16 Scott, op. cit., p. 40.
17 Polanyi, *Personal Knowledge*, p. 312.
18 John Puddefoot, 'Michael Polanyi – His Aims and Methods', *Convivium* (privately published), 21 (1985), p. 6.
19 Polanyi, *Tacit Dimension*, pp. 10–11.
20 Polanyi, *Science, Faith and Society*, Oxford, Oxford University Press, 1946, p. 10; *Personal Knowledge*, pp. 303, 305.
21 Quoted J. F. Wyatt, 'Not the Pleasure of Knowing – But of Learning', *Higher Education Newsletter* (privately printed and circulated), 10 (1985), p. 6.
22 Polanyi, *Personal Knowledge*, p. 305.
23 Joan Crewdson, summarising Polanyi's thought in an unpublished paper on which this chapter draws heavily.
24 Martin Buber, *I and Thou*, trs. R. Gregor Smith, Edinburgh, 1937, p. 3.
25 D. Scott, review of an article by R. Brownhill in *Convivium*, 13 (1981), p. 18.
26 Crewdson (see n. 23).
27 Ibid.
28 Iris Murdoch, op. cit., p. 65.
29 Ibid, p. 40.
30 Ibid, p. 62.
31 Polanyi, *Tacit Dimension*, p. 78.
32 Polanyi, *Personal Knowledge*, p. 150.
33 Polanyi, *Science, Faith and Society*, pp. 82–3.
34 Brian Cox, 'Product Balance', *Higher Education Newsletter*, 14 (1987), p. 11.
35 R. Hodgkin, quoting Polanyi, *Convivium*, 13 (1981), p. 16.
36 Polanyi, *Personal Knowledge*, pp. 204–22.

Chapter 3

1 Quoted by C. C. Gillispie, *The Edge of Objectivity*, Princeton, University Press, 1960, p. 42.
2 Francis Bacon, *Novum Organum*, trs. R. Ellis, J. Spedding, London, Longman, n.d., Preface.
3 Ibid, Aphorisms, CXXIX, p. 148.

4 Quoted Gillispie, op. cit., p. 78.
5 Bacon, op. cit., (n. 2), Preface.
6 Quoted W. H. Armytage, *Civic Universities*, London, Benn, 1955, p. 78.
7 For the rest of this paragraph, see M. Reeves, 'The European University from Medieval Times, with special reference to Oxford and Cambridge', *Higher Education: Demand and Response*, ed. W. R. Niblett, London, Tavistock, 1969, pp. 76–7.
8 Quoted Ernest Cassirer, *The Logic of the Humanities*, trs. C. S. Howe, New Haven, Yale University Press, 1961, p. 4.
9 Bacon, *Novum Organum*, p. 70.
10 Quoted Gillispie, op. cit., p. 159.
11 Quoted F. W. Matson, *The broken image: man, science and society*, New York, Free Press, 1964, p. 33.
12 Quoted Roszak, op. cit., p. 316.
13 Quoted Theodore Roszak, *Where the Wasteland Ends*, London, Faber & Faber, 1973, pp. 324–5.
14 Percy Bysshe Shelley, *A Defence of Poetry*, ed. H. Brett-Smith, Oxford, Oxford University Press, 1945, p. 52.
15 Ibid, pp. 52–3.
16 See Reeves, op. cit., p. 82.
17 Humphrey Davy, *Discourse on Chemistry*, London, House of the Royal Institution, 1802, quoted Roszak, op. cit., p. 195.
18 Polanyi, *Personal Knowledge*, p. 59.
19 Morton Bloomfield, *Piers Plowman as a Fourteenth-century Apocalypse*, New Brunswick, Rutgers University Press, n.d., pp. xiii–xiv.
20 Arthur Koestler, *The Act of Creation*, London, Pan Books, 1970, p. 117.
21 Quoted ibid, pp. 146–7.
22 Quoted ibid, p. 264.
23 William Wordsworth, 'The Tables Turned', *The Poetical Works of William Wordsworth*, ed. E. de Selincourt, H. Darbishire, Oxford, Oxford University Press, 1947, p. 57; Polanyi, *Tacit Dimension*, p. 18.
24 Quoted Roszak, op. cit., p. 309.
25 David Martin, 'The academic disciplines and religion', *Higher Education Newsletter*, 8 (1984), p. 23.
26 Louis Dupré, ibid, p. 35.
27 Quoted Cassirer, op. cit., p. 79.
28 F. J. C. Schiller, *On the Aesthetic Education of Man*, ed. & trs. E. Wilkinson, L. Willoughby, Oxford, Oxford University Press, 1967, p. 39. In this connection Goethe's development is instructive. Turning first to the study of botany, he found Linnaeus repulsive: 'There was in Linnaeus nothing but nomenclature, nothing for the intelligence, nor the imagination, no place for loveliness of form or flower.' Then, enchanted by colours, he turned to Newton's *Opticks*, but found this as barren, an anatomizing activity, taking wholes to bits and turning 'acts into husks'. Goethe was seeking something different: to penetrate into nature rather than to analyse it objectively. Man was fundamentally not just an observer of nature but a participant in it. He did not like using instruments for observation and measurement – not even spectacles – because they separated men from nature, emphasizing their alienation and aggressiveness (see Gillispie, op. cit., pp. 193–5).
29 Quoted from *The Morality of Scholarship*, ed. M. Black, in *Education and the Development of Reason*, ed. R. Dearden, P. Hirst, R. Peters, London, Routledge & Kegan Paul, 1972, p. 490.

30 Roszak, op. cit., p. 384.
31 Stephen Medcalf, 'On reading books from a half-alien culture', *The Later Middle Ages*, ed. S. Medcalf, London, Methuen, 1981, pp. 3–4.
32 Quoted in *Education and the Development of Reason* (n. 29), p. 490.
33 Liam Hudson, *The Cult of the Fact*, London, Cape, 1972, p. 39.

Chapter 4

1 Thomas Traherne, *Centuries of Meditation*, ed. B. Dobell, Oxford, Oxford University Press, 1908, p. 28.
2 T. Roszak, *The Making of a Counter Culture*, London, Faber & Faber, 1970, p. 50.
3 Quoted ibid, p. 49.
4 J. V. Taylor, 'The Importance of not Solving the Problem', *Hockerill Foundation Lecture* (privately published), 1983, unpag.
5 Ibid.
6 Ibid.
7 Ibid.
8 Michael Oakeshott, *Rationalism in politics and other essays*, London, Methuen, 1962, pp. 198–9.
9 Quoted Richard Harris, 'Religious Education and English Literature', *Hockerill Foundation Lectures* (privately published), 1982, unpag.
10 Robert Bolt, *A Man for all Seasons*, London, Heinemann, 1960, p. xiv.
11 C. S. Lewis, op. cit. (ch. II, n. 6), p. 23.
12 Wyatt, loc. cit. (ch. II, n. 21), p. 6.
13 A. J. P. Kenny, *A Path from Rome, an Autobiography*, London, Sidgewick and Jackson, 1985
14 Traherne, op. cit., pp. 156–8.
15 Ralph Townsend, unpublished sermon.
16 Ibid.
17 Traherne, op. cit., pp. 186–7.
18 Quoted Koestler, op. cit., p. 260.
19 Melvyn Matthews, 'Learning and Spirituality', *Higher Education Newsletter*, 10 (1985), p. 38.
20 Murdoch, op. cit., p. 56.
21 Nicholas Maxwell, *From Knowledge to Wisdom: A Revolution in the Aims and Methods of Science*, Oxford, Blackwell, 1984.
22 W. Langland, *Piers Plowman*, ed. W. W. Skeat, Oxford, Oxford University Press, 1886. Vol. 1, p. 3 (B. Text, Prologue, 1.17).
23 Murdoch, op. cit., pp. 58–62.
24 Koestler, op. cit., p. 260.

Chapter 5

1 Melvyn Matthews, 'Thoughts after an Oxford Conference', *Areopagus*, 15 (1984), pp. 2–3.
2 Ibid, p. 5.
3 Ibid, pp. 5–6.
4 Desmond Ryan, 'An Impermeable Membrane? Or, when will academic teaching

incorporate student learning research?', *Student learning: research in education and cognitive psychology*, ed. J. T. Richardson *et al.*, Milton Keynes, SRHE & Open University Press, 1987, p. 186. The following quotations are from pp. 187–9.

5 Ibid, pp. 190–1.
6 Memorial address on Charles Coulson.
7 Frances Stevens, 'Personal Knowledge and Poetic Imagination', *Convivium*, 14 (1982), p. 22.
8 Basil Mitchell, Discussion paper for the Pinfarthings Group.
9 Leviticus, 30: 15, 19.
10 D. E. Jenkins, 'Universe and University – Reflections on having the nerve to do theology', reprinted from *The University of Leeds Review* (1982), p. 132.
11 Goodlad, op. cit. (see ch. 1, n. 14).
12 Ibid, pp. 22, 19.

Chapter 6

1 Andrew Phillips, 'The Love of Money', Hibbert Lecture Broadcast 23/2/88, copies from the Hibbert Trust, 14 Gordon Square, London, WC1H OA9.
2 Martin Bloy, 'The Counter Culture: it just won't go away', first published in *Commonweal*, 8 October, 1971, reprinted in *Vesper Exchange* (privately printed and circulated), 8 (1972), p. 2.
3 William Bouwsma, 'Intellectual History in the 1980s', *Journal of Interdisciplinary History*, xii: 2 (1980), pp. 289–90.
4 David Jenkins, *Ecumenical Review*, xxiii (1971), pp. 160–1.
5 Michael Dummett in a conference speech.
6 Barbara Reynolds, 'Reductionism in Literary Theory', *Reductionism in Academic Disciplines*, ed. A. R. Peacocke, Guildford, SRHE & NFER, Nelson, 1985, pp. 82–4.
7 C. Nolan, *Under the Eye of the Clock*, London, Weidenfeld & Nicholson, 1987.
8 Reported by E. Braithwaite, 'Race and the Divided Self', *Frontier*, Nov., 1971, pp. 202–10.
9 Ibid, pp. 198–9.
10 Ibid, p. 209.
11 Ibid, pp. 209–10.
12 Richard Livingstone, *The Future in Education*, Cambridge, Cambridge University Press, 1941, Note and pp. 11–19.
13 Emile Rose Macaulay, *Pleasure of Ruins*, London, Weidenfeld & Nicholson, 1953.
14 A. Hastings, *A History of English Christianity from 1920 to 1985*, London, Collins, 1986.
15 Ralf Dahrendorf, 'The Underclass and the Future of Britain', Tenth Annual Lecture, St. George's House, Windsor (1987).
16 Ibid, p. 7.
17 Ibid, p. 9.
18 Michael Dummett (n. 5 above). A scheme announced in March, 1986 for a Credit Accumulation and Transfer Scheme (CATS), by which a degree can be built up by taking units in several institutions exemplifies several features touched on here: the use of a 'module' system to build up 'personal courses'; the recognition of 'experience' as a component in adult education; the call for flexibility and interchange between institutions on Higher Education. The hope is that this scheme will 'open up higher education to a whole range of people who have hitherto been put off by it, or have not known about it, or have felt it was not for them' (*The Times*, 22/3/86).

Chapter 7

1   Francis Drake (ed.) with introduction by W. S. W. Vaux, *The World Encompassed* . . . , Hakluyt Society, London, 1854, Vol. 16 (reprinted New York, 1964), p. 5.

2   Cassirer, op. cit. (ch. III, n. 8), p. 58.

3   These quotations from Freire are taken from an article by W. Simpfend-Örfer, trs. E. Walter, entitled 'Paulo Freire', *Audenshaw Documents*, 31, privately printed and circulated by the Audenshaw Foundation.

4   Quoted T. M. Roszak, *The Making of a Counter Culture*, London, 1970, p. 245.

5   Wordsworth, *The Prelude*, Bk. I, ll. 562–4.

6   Quoted Roszak, *Where the Wasteland Ends*, p. 177.

7   Alasdair Macintyre, *After Virtue. A Study in moral theory*, London, Duckworth, 1981, p. 31.

8   Ibid, p. 175.

9   Ibid, p. 177.

10 Ibid, p. 178.

11 See J. Crewdson, review of A. Milanec, *To Empower as Jesus did: Acquiring Power through Apprenticeship*, New York/Toronto, 1982, in *Convivium*, 15 (1982), p. 7.

12 Macintyre, op. cit., pp. 203, 206–7.

13 Gabrielle Taylor, 'Integrity', *The Aristotelian Society*, supplementary vol. IV (1981), pp. 144–5.

14 Ibid, p. 145.

15 Ibid, p. 149

16 Macintyre, op. cit., p. 240.

17 Taylor, loc. cit., p. 156.

18 Jenkins, 'Universe and University' (see ch. V, n. 10), p. 130.

19 Ibid, pp. 130–1.

20 Ibid, p. 131.

21 The title of a seventeenth-century pamphlet by John Saltmarsh (London, 1648).

22 L. Carroll, *Through the Look Glass and what Alice Found There*, *The Complete Works of Lewis Carroll*, London, n.d., Nonesuch Press, p. 196.

23 Stevens, loc. cit., p. 16.

24 From 'Ode on a Grecian Urn'.

25 Murdoch, op. cit., p. 55.

26 D. H. Lawrence, *The Plumed Serpent*, London, Heinemann, 1955, p. 439.

27 Geoffrey Price, 'Universities today: between the corporate state and the market', *Universities Quarterly: Culture, Education and Society*, 39:1 (Winter 1984–5), p. 51.

28 Quoted ibid, p. 52.

29 Ibid, pp. 52–3.

30 Gillian Evans, *Old Arts and New Theology – the beginnings of theology as an academic discipline*, Oxford, Oxford University Press, 1980, p. 93.

31 Jenkins, 'Universe and University', p. 135.

32 Ibid, pp. 135–6.

33 J. Milton, *Lycidas*, line 125.

34 Stephen Prickett, 'Education as Failure', *Higher Education Newsletter*, 6 (1983), p. 14.

35 Stephen Prickett, 'Has Liberalism a Future?', *Higher Education Newsletter*, 7 (1984), p. 49.

36 W. H. Owen, *Journey from Obscurity, Memoirs of the Owen Family*, London, Oxford University Press, 1963–5.

37 Dante, *Purgatorio*, XXVII, ll, 139–142.

38 A. M. Allchin, 'Celebration', *Sobornost*, series 6, 5 (1973), p. 308.
39 Ibid, pp. 309–10.
40 Ibid, p. 300.
41 Ibid.
42 Ibid, pp. 312–15.
43 D. Nicholl, 'Fyodorov', *Sobornost*, loc. cit., pp. 300–7.
44 Ibid, p. 305.
45 Ibid.
46 Matthews, loc. cit., p. 23.
47 Ibid, p. 24, quoting Brian Thorne, 'Can a University Care?' *Areopagus*, 13 (1983).

Index

The Society for Research into Higher Education

The Society exists both to encourage and co-ordinate research and development into all aspects of Higher Education, including academic, organizational and policy issues; and also to provide a forum for debate, verbal and printed. Through its activities, it draws attention to the significance of research into, and development in, HigherEducation and to the needs of scholars in this field. (It is not concerned with research generally, except, for instance, as a subject of study.)

The Society's income derives from subscriptions, book sales, conferences and specific grants. It is wholly independent. Its corporate members are institutions of higher education, research institutions and professional, industrial, and governmental bodies. Its individual members include teachers and researchers, administrators and students. Members are found in all parts of the world and the Society regards its international work as amongst its most important activities.

The Society discusses and comments on policy, organizes conferences and encourages research. Under the Imprint SRHE & OPEN UNIVERSITY PRESS, it is a specialist publisher, having some 40 titles in print. It also publishes *Studies in Higher Education* (three times a year) which is mainly concerned with academic issues, *Higher Education Quarterly* (formerly *Universities Quarterly*) which will be mainly concerned with policy issues, *Research into Higher Education Abstracts* (three times a year), and a *Bulletin* (six times a year).

The Society's committees, study groups and branches are run by members (with help from a small staff at Guildford), and aim to provide a form for discussion. The groups at present include a Teacher Education Study Group, a Staff Development Group, a Women in Higher Education Group and a Continuing Education Group which may have had their own organization, subscriptions or publications; (eg the *Staff Development Newsletter*). The Governing Council, elected by members, comments on current issues; and discusses policies with leading figures, notably at its evening Forums. The Society organizes seminars on current research for officials of DES and other ministries, an Anglo-American series on standards, and is in touch with bodies in the UK such as the NAB, CVCP, UGC, CNAA and the British Council, and with sister-bodies overseas. Its current research projects include one on the relationship between entry qualifications and degree results, directed by Prof. W. D. Furneaux (Brunel) and one on questions of quality directed by Prof. G. C. Moodie (York). A project on the evaluation of the research standing of university departments is in preparation. The Society's conferences are often held jointly. Annual Conferences have considered 'Professional Education' (1984), 'Continuing Education' (1985, with Goldsmiths' College) 'Standards and Criteria in Higher Education' (1986, with Bulmershe CHE), 'Restructuring' (1987, with the City of Birmingham Polytechnic) and 'Academic Freedom' (1988, the University of

Surrey). Other conferences have considered the DES 'Green Paper' (1985, with the Times Higher Education Supplement), and 'The First-Year Experience' (1986, with the University of South Carolina and Newcastle Polytechnic). For some of the Society's conferences, special studies are commissioned in advance, as 'Precedings'.

Members receive free of charge the Society's *Abstracts*, annual conference Proceedings (or 'Precedings'), *Bulletin and International Newsletter* and may buy SRHE & OPEN UNIVERSITY PRESS books at booksellers' discount. Corporate members also receive the Society's journal *Studies in Higher Education* free (individuals at a heavy discount). They may also obtain *Evaluation Newsletter* and certain other journals at a discount, including the NFER *Register of Educational Research*. There is a substantial discount to members, and to staff of corporate members, on annual and some other conference fees.